Coping with

D0004925

GRIEVING AND LOSS

Sandra and Owen Giddens

THE ROSEN PUBLISHING GROUP, INC.
NEW YORK

To Justine and Kyle, and in loving memory of Denise, Cynthia, Christabel, Andrew, Janis, Jean-Marc, Vijay, and Bruce

Published in 2000 by The Rosen Publishing Group, Inc.
29 East 21st Street, New York, NY 10010

Copyright © 2000 by Sandra and Owen Giddens

First Edition

Library of Congress Cataloging-in-Publication Data
Giddens, Sandra.
    Coping with grieving and loss / Sandra and Owen Giddens.
        p. cm. (Coping)
    Includes bibliographical references and index.
    Summary: Explains the stages of grieving and how to cope with loss and death, including where to go for help.
    ISBN 0-8239-2894-2 (lib. bdg.)
    1. Grief in adolescence—Juvenile literature. 2. Bereavement in adolescence—Juvenile literature. 3. Loss (Psychology) in adolescence—Juvenile literature. 4. Teenagers and death—Juvenile literature. [1. Grief. 2. Death. 3. Loss (Psychology).] I. Giddens, Owen. II. Series.
    BF724.3.G73 .G53   1999
    155.9'37'0835—dc21   99-044890
                                                CIP
                                                AC

Manufactured in the United States of America

About the Authors

Owen Giddens, Ph.D., C.S.W., L.M.F.C.C., is in private practice as a psychotherapist, helping teens to work through the grieving process. He works with both individuals and families and specializes in pain management techniques. Owen is married to Sandra Giddens, and they have two children, Justine and Kyle.

Sandra Giddens, M.Ed., is currently an educational assessment teacher with the Toronto District School Board. Her first book, *Escape: Teens Who Escaped from the Holocaust to Freedom,* was published by the Rosen Publishing Group in January 1999. Sandra is presently working on her Doctorate of Education dissertation. She would like to dedicate this book to the loving memory of her father, Joe Weisfeld.

Acknowledgments

Special thanks to Rabbi Larry Pinsker, Pastor Bob Fukimoto, and Dr. Leslie Balmer.

Contents

Introduction

We live in a world where endings in fairy tales conclude with "They lived happily ever after." When you were a child you may have wanted to live in that fantasy world. As you grow older and gain more life experience, you soon come to realize that life begins with birth, and death will eventually follow.

A long time ago in a small village, a woman came to the religious leader. In her arms she tightly gripped a small bundle. She begged for an audience before the leader. When it was finally granted, she pleaded with the leader to bring her small baby back to life. The leader compassionately told her that she must look into the eyes of others in the village to find a family that had never been touched by death. The woman wandered the village day and night and looked into peoples' eyes and heard their stories. She finally returned to the leader. She said that she now was ready to bury her baby. She understood that death had touched everyone at one time or another.

As you watch the different stages that a flower goes through, from seed to bud, to full bloom, and finally to wilting, you will also see the different stages of your own life. If you were to live a long life you would grow from infant to child, to teenager, to adult, and finally to old age. Each

1

stage would bring its own beauty and wisdom. Just as living has its stages, so does the process of dying.

Dying is a difficult concept to understand. One of the most profound changes that can happen to a young person is the death of a loved one and the immense sense of loss and grieving that follows. Death has knocked at everyone's door. Although you may not want to answer it, it eventually comes for everyone. The author Chaim Potok, in his book *My Name Is Asher Lev*, tells of a young boy named Asher who has a conversation with his father about death. The young Asher and his father are walking home from Sabbath services when the boy sees a bird lying next to the curb.

"Is it dead, Papa?" I was six and could not bring myself to look at it.

"Yes," I heard him say in a sad and distant way.

"Why did it die?"

"Everything that lives must die."

"Everything?"

"Yes."

"And me?"

"Yes," he said. Then he added in Yiddish, "But may it be only after you live a long and good life, my Asher."

I could not grasp it. I forced myself to look at the bird. Everything alive would some day be still as the bird?

"Why?" I asked.

"That's the way the Ribbonon Shelolom made his world, Asher."

"Why?"

"So life would be precious, Asher. Something that is yours forever is never precious."

Each culture through the ages has tried to comprehend death in its own way. Understanding cultural and individual differences in beliefs about death can build bridges to understanding common human values. Many cultures believe that everyone has a soul or spirit and that the soul or spirit lives on after death. Some believe that the spirit goes up to heaven to be with God, and others believe that the spirit takes a new form on earth. There are individuals who believe that there is nothing after death. Christians envision the road to eternal life as a central focus in their religion. Protestants feel that God accompanies a person both in life and death. Eternal life in heaven will be more readily achieved if one has loved God. Catholics see death as God's will and regard the attainment of eternal life as a goal that shapes their behavior. Often Jewish people rely on the justice of God's ways and emphasize living well and leaving themselves in God's hands. Followers of many Eastern religions believe in the immortality of the soul.

The beliefs of both eastern and western religious groups have shaped our views of the unique dignity and worthiness of each living being, and made the death of any being an event of importance. Whether you follow a religious path or not, the death of a loved one does have a profound effect on you.

Dr. Elisabeth Kübler-Ross worked and cared for chronically ill patients. Through her experiences, she began to see that her dying patients went through five stages in relationship to their own process of dying.

3

- Shock and denial (*No, not me.*)

- Anger (*Why me?*)

- Bargaining (*If I will do this, then. . .*)

- Depression

- Acceptance

Anyone who has suffered the death of a loved one can also go through many or all of these stages during his or her grieving period. These stages do not necessarily come in any order. They can exist at different times and can last for varying lengths of time. Some teenagers will not experience a certain stage and others will remain in one stage for a long time. These stages reflect coping mechanisms that provide a person with a way to deal with loss.

It is important for you to understand that you are unique. How you cope and how you go through the grieving process may be very similar to or very different from that of your best friend or other family members.

What Is Loss, Grieving, and Mourning?

Loss is an experience that you live and grow with. Some losses can be considered in a positive light, like a move to a new home. You may feel the loss of your old house and neighborhood, yet you may be moving to a better neighborhood and bigger home. Graduation from high school may be considered a loss of part of your youth, yet it is positive because you are moving on toward adulthood and further responsibilities. Some losses are difficult to deal with, as when you break up with a girlfriend or boyfriend. When parents separate and divorce, there is a feeling of great loss.

Losses that occur without much warning can often leave the teenager without the strategies to cope. Even losses that are anticipated can still leave the teenager overwhelmed and unable to cope. Each loss must be faced, worked through, and managed in a healthy way. The way one copes with loss may indicate how one copes with life. One of the greatest feelings of loss is the death of a loved one.

Grief

Grief can be defined as the combination of thoughts and feelings you experience about a loss. The death of a pet may be your first introduction to the grieving process. This may bring a deep feeling of grief. Grief is not a disorder, a disease, or a sign of weakness. It is an indication of your humanity and connectedness to other people. Grief often makes people feel as if they are losing control. Grief can manifest itself in many ways: crying, sleeplessness, lack of appetite, and recurring painful thoughts. The only cure for grief is to grieve. You won't be feeling this sad for the rest of your life. Grieving comes and goes. At times you will feel that you are riding the wave and at other times you may feel that you are drowning. You may feel sad, then fine for a few months, then experience sadness again. Scott Sullender, in his book *Grief and Growth,* states that:

> *The griever's suffering is never constant. The waves of pain are alternated by lulls of momentary rest. Initially, of course, in acute grief situations the waves are intense and frequent. Gradually, as one is healed, the waves are less intense, less prolonged and less frequent. . . Gradually, ever so gradually, the storm quiets. Yet months and years later an isolated wave can still come crashing ashore.*

Mourning

When you mourn, you take the grief that is inside you and express it externally. When will you feel better? No one can give you that answer. There is no timetable for how long you will hurt or feel sad. You can't measure grief in terms of a calendar. It is important to allow yourself to heal at your own individual pace. Each person mourns in his or her own special way. You may not cope in the same way as other members of your family or your friends. Each person that we interviewed handled loss, grieving, and mourning in their own unique way. How you handle the grieving process depends on many personal factors:

- ⮑ Your relationship to the person who died
- ⮑ Your coping strategies
- ⮑ The support you receive from others
- ⮑ The circumstances surrounding the death

There is no good time to encounter death, but the teenage years are a very difficult time to cope with the loss of a loved one. This is the time when the teenager is finding and asserting his or her own independence and individuality. This is the stage when the teen feels powerful and free of cares. The loss of a loved one disrupts the teen's feeling of immortality and threatens his or her sense of security.

Together we shall now take a journey as seen through the eyes and experiences of a number of teenagers who have experienced the death of a loved one. We will learn their reactions to loss and see how they went through the grieving process. We will endeavor to help by sharing some of the methods that these teenagers used in coping with the death of their loved ones. We will also examine some techniques suggested by experts who help teenagers with the grieving process.

Before the Death, I Remember . . .

As a teenager a young person feels the need to separate from adult authority. Teens gravitate toward and identify with people of their own age. They may experience mood swings. They may begin dating. A teenager may feel care-free, with few burdens and responsibilities. Developmentally, the teenage years are a difficult time to encounter the death of a loved one. This is a forward-thinking time for young people. It is the time that teens are asserting their own independence and autonomy, and moving away from the nuclear family. The loss of a loved one at this age deeply violates their need to feel powerful, in control, free of intense cares, and immortal.

Death has a way of altering your perceptions about life. As complex as your life has been, with the death of a loved one it now becomes more complex. As a teenager you may have not thought too much about death or tried to avoid thinking about it. This naivete may leave you feeling more vulnerable when a death actually occurs. You may feel overburdened and overwhelmed. You wonder if you will ever go back to being just a regular teenager again. In his book *Bereavement: Counseling the Grieving Throughout the Life Cycle*, David Crenshaw says:

> *No one ever completely recovers from the loss of someone they deeply loved. Recovery from grief means you can face and bear the loss, but you are permanently changed as a result of the experience. Some of these changes may be positive as we may gain or discover strength within ourselves.*

The impact of death can be so profound that a teenager will view his or her own life as divided between preloss and postloss periods. Teens see themselves in a certain light before the death of a loved one and after the death they may view themselves in a different light.

Before my sister's death I was shy and kept to myself. Now I am more outgoing. — Kelvin

Before the suicide of my brother, I remember being happy all the time. I was enthusiastic, always making jokes, but now I am more quiet. — Alex

Before my brother's death I was irresponsible. I just wanted to have fun. Now I argue more with my parents and I am drifting. — Mike

Most teenagers have never experienced the death of a loved one. When the event occurs, it leaves a profound and long-lasting effect. Some teens see themselves as having to grow up faster, almost as if they had lost a part of their youth or childhood. Others see themselves as learning from the event, and their personalities change because of the death. Final memories of a loved one can be pivotal in changing one's viewpoint about life.

Most teenagers vividly remember the last significant event that happened to them before a person's death. It could have been a conversation, an event, or a feeling. The last memory can make a lifelong impression in the mind of a teenager.

I remember Mom sitting in the front hallway and she was sitting on Dad's lap. She looked so cute. I remember thinking they were such a good couple together. It was not fair. — Meghan

I remember the last conversation with my brother. He was laughing about being in a fight. He was laughing about it. He was silly that way. — Mike

I remember my father saying, "This must be hard on you." I responded, "Don't worry about me. I'm fine. I'm fine." — Sarah

I remember our spaghetti meal together. I kept kissing him on the cheek and he wanted me to stop. We were fooling around at the table and then we went to watch TV. Our last time could have been a fight but it was not and I am glad about that. — Nina

I remember the last time we were together, we fought over the TV and I called her a bitch. I regret that to this day. — Kelvin

I remember she went to the hospital. I couldn't go. I didn't want to see her in pain. I felt it was a good choice not to go. — Matthew

The reactions to the death of a loved one can vary. Some teenagers may feel that they are prepared to deal with the worst. They believe that they have had time to adjust to the loss of someone with a long-term illness, such as a parent dying of cancer. But when the death actually occurs, they feel numb and in shock. There is a sense of unreality to the situation. When there is a sudden death, as in a car accident, a murder, or a suicide, there is also a sense of unreality to the situation.

My mother was a teacher who was well loved by her students. I remember before she got sick we would cuddle together on the couch. When they told me she had cancer, I couldn't believe it. I never thought she would die. — Matthew

My mother told me that she and my father were going to get divorced. I was relieved. My father was depressed. He kept on staring at us from the doorway. My brother kept on insisting that we should leave and get away. The day Mom and I came home from the optometrist, I discovered that my house was on fire. Later on I was told that my father had slit my brother's throat with a knife and then set fire to himself and the house. I am still haunted by the scenes in my head of my brother's last actions before he was so brutally murdered. — Nina

The summer before my brother died, he was on the computer constantly, talking on a chat line. The day he committed suicide, I kept on watching him go back and forth to the garage. I never suspected he would kill himself. — Alex

I remember dinnertime, eating together as a family. Then Mom was killed in a car accident. Now we share a meal without her. It isn't the same. — Krystal

11

At the moment teenagers find out that a loved one has died, they may go into a state of shock, terror, fear, or disbelief. Sometimes there is denial that the event even occurred.

When I saw Dad's body, I thought, you must be kidding, this cannot be happening. I kept expecting him to blink. I kept thinking it was a joke. — Sarah

My parents came in to tell me that my brother had died. I rolled over and went back to sleep. I felt it must be a dream. When I woke up and realized the truth, I just wanted to be by myself. — Mike

I thought I was sleeping. It did not seem real. — Alex

Denial does not make the pain go away. Denial is one way to keep the pain inside until you are ready to deal with it. The pain and knowledge of what has just occurred may seem insurmountable at the time. Your sense of sadness may be overpowering and you may just want to cry. Others become silent and remove themselves from the situation, sometimes able to cry and sometimes not. Sometimes the tears are only inside.

I cried a little but not much. I was in shock. — Sarah

I broke down, and then we sat there and I did not know what to say. — Meghan

Sometimes teenagers are living lives before a death that are filled with stress. They may be coping with a parent with an illness, a depressed sibling, or parents who are divorcing. They find it difficult to go out every day and act normally. They wonder why their lives are filled with this pain and sadness while others appear to be so happy. When death occurs they sometimes wonder if they will ever feel joy and happiness again.

I took care of Dad. I gave him his medication, gave him food when he could eat, and helped him when he was mobile. — Sarah

The cancer came back. It had spread to her back and lungs. She was at home with a hospital bed and nurses doing dressings. I felt very sad. I was into avoidance. — Tasha

Dad told me that Mom's cancer was back. I never thought she would die. I never thought death would touch me. — Meghan

My mom told me they were getting a divorce. I was totally shocked. My brother was really upset. Six months in the house was hell. — Nina

Other teenagers have rarely experienced severe pressure and stress in their lives. When the death occurs, they can be devastated by these new emotions.

We used to decorate our house for occasions. We made a big deal about it. I miss everything about her. — Karla

My brother is always in the back of my mind. — Nina

When the knowledge of the death of a loved one sinks in, there is no psychological preparation for the news. The best coping mechanism is to allow yourself to express your feelings. Let yourself feel the emotional turmoil. It is all right to cry and it is all right not to cry.

Some teenagers may benefit from counseling before a death occurs. This could be helpful when a loved one in the family is dying and the whole household is affected. Through counseling, teens will receive help in dealing with their feelings of losing the person they love. They can also be counseled in finding a good way to say goodbye to their loved ones. Many teenagers feel that they do not want to be around the person who is dying, as it creates many emotions that they are not prepared to deal with at the time. A counselor can help teenagers work through their feelings of dealing with the impending death of their loved one.

It was very important for the teenagers that we interviewed to have an opportunity to say "I love you" to the person who was dying. If they did not say "I love you," they felt there was something missing. They needed closure and many did not have the opportunity to receive it.

I gave her a big hug and told her I loved her. I don't know why, something told me to, an urge. In the hospital I held her and kissed her. I knew she could hear me. Something inside me told me she could.
—Meghan

The night before she died, a family member put the phone to her ear and I told her I loved her. She told me that she loved me, too. — Tasha

At the wake, I held her hand and kissed her. — Matthew

But all the preparation in the world does not prepare anyone for the feelings that occur at the funeral of a loved one.

The Funeral

The funeral is an opportunity to come together with others who are touched by the death of a loved one. Together you share in the experience and together you help each other to remember the person who died. A funeral allows you to publicly cry. Some teenagers may have been brought up with the understanding that it is not right to cry in public. A funeral is a time when tears are allowed and accepted. A funeral is also a time where you may see other family members, who usually have their emotions under control, now appear heartbroken.

I never saw Dad cry. It was the first time.
— Meghan

I worried about Mom and Dad. Mom looked like she was going to lose it. — Mike

A funeral is also a time for emotional upheaval. You may be feeling anger for having this happen to you personally. You may fear for the future, and feel pain for having to undergo this turbulence in your life.

Everyone was hugging. I was trying to get away from everyone to be by myself. — Krystal

The priest conducted the funeral. My brother's girl-friend lay down a white rose. I wandered off. People were everywhere, but I did not want to talk. I wanted to leave. I sobbed at the cemetery. — Mike

I put flowers on the casket, stayed there in the rain, and leaned down the hole to say goodbye. — Kelvin

At the burial I told myself I was going to be strong. I told myself I wasn't going to cry. I didn't cry at the funeral. I cried when I got home. — Karla

I was crying. Her spirit had gone to heaven and her body was there. — Matthew

He was buried in a nice place under a tree, on a nice sunny day. I stood there and cried. I was really blank and scared, and I didn't know what was going to happen now. — Alex

I drove down to the cemetery and was over-whelmed by all the people. It was cold outside. They lowered the coffin and the pastor said a prayer. I stood watching, feeling helpless. There was nothing I could do about this. I did not want to leave. I did not remember the whole funeral. — Meghan

Dad had planned his own funeral. There were psalms and Jim Morrison songs. I did not act how I was supposed to. I was sometimes smiling and laugh-ing when it was inappropriate. — Sarah

I was strong at the funeral, until the burial. Then I broke down. — Tasha

Many Christian funerals are preceded by a wake. The wake is often held in a funeral home. The purpose of the wake is to unite people who want to pay their respects and offer condolences to the relatives who are mourning. The coffin may be either opened or closed. For some teenagers, this may be the first time that they view the body of their loved one.

He did not look real. He looked like he was sleeping. I felt that the situation was unreal. I could not believe it. — Alex

I felt I never really looked at her. I almost did not recognize her. — Kelvin

Her body was there but her soul was in my heart. — Matthew

I went up to the casket and started to feel delirious. I had to get some air. — Mike

I knew it was the last time I would see her. — Meghan

It was not her when I kissed her. It was so cold and hard. — Karla

If I hadn't seen my brother, I thought I always might want to. I think I wanted to put some closure to it. — Nina

Not all bodies are buried. Some people's last request is to have their bodies cremated. There is still a funeral service. The ashes may be scattered or placed in an urn that is then put in a special place.

They took the bodies into a side room and they went into ovens. Mom turned my brother's knob and my uncle turned my father's knob. — Nina

Dad was cremated and his ashes were put into a memory box. — Sarah

As a teenager, this may be the first time you attend a funeral. You may not know what is expected of you. It is helpful to have some understanding of the sequence of events at a funeral so that there is some familiarity with what is going to happen. It is also important to understand that the emotions you will feel may be new to you. Many people go into a state of shock when attending a funeral. There is such a state of unreality and grief connected with this experience that some people claim they walked through the events and have no memory of them afterward. Some people feel as if they are in a painting and they are viewing the events almost like an outsider. The shock of death sometimes makes people feel that their minds are frozen. This may be nature's way of helping you to cope so that you will not be emotionally overwhelmed.

When they lowered my mother into the ground, I broke down and cried. She was not coming back. I felt like I wanted to go with her. — Tasha

I looked around at all the people and saw lots of people I did not know. I was totally freaked out by all the people. I was in a daze, completely numb. — Mike

I was scared at what was going to happen now. He was gone. I will never have a brother again. — Alex

I felt that my mom's spirit had gone to heaven. — Matthew

I wished at the funeral that I could see her one more time. — Karla

I don't remember a lot. I blanked out a few times. I was confused. One moment billions of things were passing through my head, another moment nothing. — Krystal

The day of the funeral started out really nice, then it started to rain really hard. The rain stopped and I could see a rainbow. In my mind it was a perfect funeral. — Kelvin

Some teenagers feel in enough control that they want to say something at the funeral service. They may have written a poem or a speech or a dedication. Some teenagers are too overwhelmed and they cannot face all the people or recite a passage.

I could not say anything at the funeral service. I was too emotional. — Meghan

I participated in the service, reading a psalm that was a prayer for protection. — Tasha

I read a song by Jim Morrison, "Death makes angels of us all and gives us wings." — Mike

At the funeral, friends, ministers, and other family members may take part in the services. They may read a eulogy containing past memories of the deceased. Some teenagers find these memories helpful at this time. Others are too distressed and cannot concentrate on the words. It is sometimes helpful and supportive if the people who gave tributes presented them in written form to the family after the funeral. Teens can then read these passages when they are emotionally ready.

I really appreciated hearing about my mom's childhood from her brother. The stories gave me a better picture of my mom growing up. — Matthew

I listened but it did not sink in. — Kelvin

After the funeral service, many of the mourners may come over to your house. In the Jewish tradition, the funeral is held within a day or two after the death. In a traditional Jewish household, for seven days following the funeral the family of the deceased observe shiva, a period of mourning where friends and relatives come to give comfort to the mourners. Some teenagers find such a gathering of people helpful to get through the initial shock.

The hardest part was after the funeral. Not as many people were around, so the reality was starting to kick in. — Tasha

After the shock of the funeral has worn off, many teens look to their friends to help them when the reality of the loss hits hard.

Friends and Family

As a teenager, your friends are extremely important in your life. How you are seen by them is important to you. Many teenagers who have gone through the grieving process felt that it was their friends who helped them the most through this emotional turmoil. More than anything else, most teens hoped to get back to "business as usual" with their friends as soon as possible.

My friends were very supportive. They were always with me. — Nina

I keep everything inside. Most guys don't want to talk about this kind of thing. — Matthew

With friends, if I want to bring it up, I will. — Sarah

I went right back to school. It was refreshing because it gave me something to think about. I wanted friends' company but I did not want to talk to people or see their reactions. — Mike

My best friend Leah slept over the whole week and stayed with me. She was one of my best friends. She knew how I felt and really cared. — Meghan

Friends were very important to teenagers during the initial stage of shock. Having friends over or going to a friend's house generated a feeling of comfort. Even though the death involved a family member, the presence of friends was needed. Many of the teenagers we interviewed immediately gravitated to their friends when they heard the news that a loved one had died. Some went over to a friend's house right away; others slept over at a friend's house or had a friend sleep over at their home. Many received support from their friends through the telephone. When a member of the family dies, usually family and friends gather at the house to offer immediate support. Some teenagers felt the presence of so many people in the house intrusive. It made it difficult for them to grieve. Others felt a sense of belonging and caring from the family. Most teenagers liked having the immediate support of their friends.

Everyone was in it together. We all felt close as a group. — Nina

I didn't want to talk to the family. They were feeling the pain. Friends were important. — Meghan

Friends were concerned that I was drinking. — Sarah

Friends were supportive. — Kelvin

I was happy to see my friends at the funeral. — Mike

Many times, friends do not know what to say. Friends may feel close to the person who is suffering. They may also feel that they are only casual acquaintances. They may not know what response is appropriate. The most common phrase is "I'm sorry." It may be the first time a teenager has to give comfort. It may also be a teenager's first experience of someone else's death. The death may conjure up feelings of other personal losses he or she has experienced. Friends may be frightened by the notion of death. They may be frightened by the realization that if this person has died, they could also die. They may also be grieving if they had a close relationship with the person who died. If it is a personal friend who has died, they may also be going through their own stages of grief. Instead of giving comfort, they will need comforting themselves.

Generally, people do not know how to react or what to say. — Mike

It was OK for people to ask if I was OK. — Nina

They told me not to worry. But it's not OK. I do worry. Everything isn't going away. — Krystal

My best friend listened and together we could share feelings. — Meghan

Having friends at the funeral was both comforting and supportive for most teenagers. It was helpful to know that they were not alone. Although they were surrounded by family, friends were seen as a vital element in the initial stage of grieving. Having friends join together to do something special for the bereaved teenager meant a great deal.

I received a card from everyone in the grade. It made me feel good. It was one of the reasons I went back to school. — Alex

Everyone in the school signed a card. — Nina

Before I went back to school, my whole class signed a paper rose. I felt good. I still have it. — Matthew

How a friend acts toward the bereaved teenager is very important. The teenager is feeling intense sadness and pain. He or she is very vulnerable and sensitive at this point in time. Teens seem to accurately sense if their friends' concern is genuine or not.

It was funny. Someone I least expected was there for me. — Kelvin

Friends will be having a conversation and I show up and they stop. I feel they are talking about me. — Karla

I received a lot of phone calls from friends saying they were sorry. I said thanks. — Alex

Sometimes friends would say they were sorry. I never knew if they meant it. One girl, not a friend, asked if I wanted to talk, like tell her my inner feelings. That made me angry. — Sarah

If the tragedy occurred during the school year, or immediately after the summer, the bereaved teenager will return to school. Some teens return fairly quickly. They want their lives to feel normal again. Others find it difficult to face their peer group. Many teenagers reported that guidance counselors and other teachers offered support.

I felt that I went back to school too soon. I could not concentrate. Teachers were open and said to come to them if I wanted to talk. One teacher did not say he was sorry but just wanted me to get back on track with my schoolwork. That was the last thing on my mind. — Alex

Mom spoke to the principal. I did not talk to anyone. — Kelvin

I don't remember the first day back at school. Friends were the same. It was business as usual. — Matthew

I went to school the first day after the funeral. I wanted to stay at school because people would be all over the house. — Mike

After the incident, I did not go back to school for the remainder of the term. Some people did not know how to approach me. They were in shock. — Nina

At times it may be difficult, but it is important for bereaved teenagers to return to school. It creates the sense that things are returning to normal. Those teenagers who received help through the guidance counseling department felt that they had a person to talk to when their emotions made it too difficult to sit in class or attend to their studies. Although some teachers were understanding, many did not know how the grieving process would affect a teenager academically and emotionally. Some teens found that their concentration level and the atmosphere at home made it difficult for them to study. Some of the teens found that it was difficult for them to achieve the same grades they had before the death of a family member. Others seemed to handle the day-to-day routine of academic life much more easily.

I am frustrated with myself. I can't pull the marks off that I used to. — Nina

My grades never dropped. — Tasha

Friends are an important part of your day-to-day existence. It is important for you to understand your own coping mechanisms. If you feel that it is helpful to talk with your friends, then do, and if you feel that talking with your friends is not your style, then don't. It may be important for you to talk with an outsider, such as a psychiatrist, a social worker, a psychologist, or a minister. Some of the teenagers we talked to found the counseling experience beneficial to them. Others found they were not ready to seek professional help and wanted to work out their grief independently.

Going to a psychiatrist, it helps. — Matthew

I did not benefit from the psychiatry. I didn't want to talk to someone when I was upset. — Nina

Although we interviewed teenagers who had lost an immediate family member, there is also an intense feeling of loss when a friend dies. When a personal friend dies, it is an unbelievable shock to the teenager. The whirlwind of emotions is paralyzing. There are also feelings of shock, denial, anger, guilt, and depression. Death can feel threatening. When a death occurs at school, friends may gather together and look for someone to blame. Teachers or administrators can be likely targets. Teens may also blame themselves. Teenagers may feel responsible for a friend's death, for example, if they knew that the friend was into drugs or was depressed. When a friend dies, there is no preparation for the onslaught of emotions.

It will often seem as if there is no reason why such a young person has had his or her life cut so short. The anger one feels is natural. The pain and sadness are part of the grieving process. It is often helpful to return to your normal activities as soon as possible, however difficult that may appear to be. Some schools have guidance counselors to offer assistance. If a large number of people are affected, there may be trauma teams that come into the school to assist both students and staff members. Remember you are not alone in your grief. There are others to share your sorrow with you and help you get through your inner pain.

I now know friends who have had people they care about die from cancer. I go up to them and tell them I know how you feel. — Meghan

Even though you think you can understand other people's pain, many times you do not discuss your own pain with your immediate family members. The way in which teenagers work through their grief depends a great deal on how family members and friends reach out to them. The more they are encouraged to share their grief, the more likely they will be able to cope with the loss in their lives.

Dealing with Family Members

As a teenager, you soon realize that the pain you are feeling is your own personal pain. You may feel as though you are on an isolated island where no one sees or understands what you are going through and experiencing. You may be surrounded by family, but feelings of loneliness may still occupy your thoughts. You may be watching other family members going through the grieving process and may not relate to them in a positive manner. You need your own time to heal. It is all right to be focused on your own needs for a while. The teenagers we interviewed felt that the family dynamics had changed after a death in the family. When a sibling dies and you are left all alone, this situation may leave you the sole focus of your parents' anger, confusion, and guilt. You may be the sole focus of their love as well. Your parents may become overprotective.

Just as you see your life as divided between pre- and post-loss periods, your relationship with your parents may also have altered. Before the death, your parents may have acted or responded in one way and now they act differently.

My parents were divorced for a long time. I also had my father's wife to deal with. My mother and I have always had a love-hate relationship. She is a talker and I like to keep my feelings to myself. When my dad died, Mom felt that I was choosing my dad's wife over her. I wondered who should be more upset, the one who lost her husband or the one who lost her ex-husband. I am trying to understand. — Sarah

My parents argue on and off with me. My brother and I agreed on a lot of things. We could talk together. Now it is just my parents and I. — Mike

I was Daddy's little girl before Mom's death. — Tasha

I still do not share my emotions with my mom and dad. — Kelvin

I don't talk to Dad as much. I am more quiet with him. There are more fights now over stupid things because I am the only one in the house. — Alex

Change also occurs in the relationship between siblings after a death in the family. The remaining sibling survivors may take on new roles, becoming mothers and fathers to the younger children. Brothers and sisters may become closer together or further apart.

My brother and I tell each other everything. He closes himself in and I get things out of him. — Meghan

I talk to my sister now. — Matthew

Sandra, my sister, was like a mother figure to me. I went to her for everything. — Tasha

My brother and I were always really close. The legal stuff from the will is putting a strain on our relationship. — Sarah

It is difficult putting yourself into your parents' shoes. They are watching you grieve and they are grieving as well. Parents are going through their own stages of grief. They may also be experiencing feelings of guilt, anger, denial, and depression. Their stages of grieving may not coincide with yours. They may not understand your mood swings as you may not understand theirs. They may also be very sad and in pain. Just as you have returned to school, your parents may have returned to work. The only time that they can feel at ease with their mourning may be when they are at home. You may not be feeling sympathetic to each other's needs.

Your mother may have lost your father or your father may have lost your mother. This may be the first time that your parent has had to approach life all alone in many years. A single parent has to adjust to a new role, and he or she may be overwhelmed by new obligations. A single parent has to take on a new role in the household, one you both will have to adjust to.

Mom had to deal with lawyers, insurance agents, detectives, and telephone calls. Mom was real strong. She also had to deal with funeral arrangements.
— Nina

I want to make sure Dad is happy. I don't want for him to be alone. — Meghan

You may be taking on roles that your mother or father used to fulfill when she or he were alive. You may be now responsible for the cooking, shopping, or dealing with financial problems. You may be feeling way over your head with all your new obligations. You may feel burdened and therefore resentful toward the surviving parent.

You may be talking to friends and not communicating with your parents. Your parents may be feeling hurt that you are reaching out to friends and not to them. Some parents feel that they are being ignored and they don't know how to reconnect with their teenager. The family dynamics have changed. It is important to understand that new dynamics will evolve. This may occur when the surviving family members reach out to each other and establish new relationships that can bridge the gap in the family structure.

I was always close to Mom. Now we are closer.
— Nina

My grandma is so good, she does a lot of stuff around the house. Otherwise I would have to take care of things like dishes and laundry. Dad and I are close but we fight a lot. My mom was the peace-keeper and now she is gone. — Meghan

One common emotion after such a loss is anger. Anger is more acceptable or tolerated in the household and not as tolerated in the school environment or out in the community.

Anger, Guilt, and Depression

The feeling of anger often comes after someone has died. There may be the desire to blame others for the death of the loved one. Some blame God for taking away a family member. Others blame themselves. There may even be an irrational desire to blame the person who has died. Why did the person have to pass away at this time and why did he or she have to leave you feeling these uncontrollable emotions? Anger is a typical response to the unexpected loss of control over one's life.

The feeling of anger can come at any time during the grieving process. Anger can be short-lived or it can remain for a longer period of time. Some people express no anger and others are filled with rage. Some teenagers feel that they can internalize their anger and others feel that letting loose and hitting an object like a pillow is a good outlet for their rage. Some are in control of their angry outbursts and others are not.

The death of a loved one is seen by a teenager as premature, before the expected time. Teens view themselves as having lost the future years with a parent or sibling. Their loved ones will not be there when they graduate from high school, get married, or have children. As well, their parents will not be there when they are feeling troubled, in pain, or in need of parental guidance. They feel that parents are not supposed to die when there are children to love and protect. Brothers and sisters are not supposed to die before they are grown adults. Bereaved teens cannot fathom a family unit without their siblings. They cannot imagine holidays without their brothers or sisters. All their dreams and plans of the future have been destroyed. Teens may feel cheated. They may be looking for someone to blame.

I was angry at everything. I was angry with God for taking my mother away from me. — Meghan

The anger is still there, but it's not as much as before. I hold in the anger. — Alex

I felt angry. Why did this happen to me? Of everybody in the world, why did this happen to me? — Matthew

Although anger after a death is considered normal and natural, difficulties arise when there is no good place to express it. If there is no deserving target, the anger can spill out at school, at home, or at unexpected times.

When I get angry, I punch my pillow. — Matthew

I get mad at my friends who talk badly about their moms. — Karla

The anger is internal. — Kelvin

I get angry at TV worlds because there are no perfect TV worlds. They are fake. — Karla

Sometimes teenagers feel angry at the person who died. It may not be a logical response to bereavement, but these teens are feeling that they have been abandoned and that their whole lives have been turned upside down. Whether death occurs naturally or violently, anger for teenagers is justified.

> *I was really mad at my brother and what he did. He did not think before he did it. He did not think of what he left behind. He did not ask for help.* — Alex

> *I was angry toward the press. Some of the articles were graphic and contained misquotes. A neighbor was interviewed and he didn't even know us!* — Nina

In the case of drunk driving, there is strong anger at the person who killed the loved one. Even if the case comes to trial, there is a feeling that the sentence, if there is one, will not be long enough. It may make you feel robbed and victimized twice. First, because the loved one's life has been needlessly taken, and second, because the guilty person has not been punished enough in your opinion.

When there is a car accident, there is also strong blame placed on the person who caused the death of the loved one. In both these cases, anger may remain with the bereaved teenager for a lengthy period of time. It may never entirely disappear. In a flash, the life of the bereaved teen has been changed. The person who was the cause of the accident is the target of the teen's anger and internal pain. It is natural to feel hatred and bitterness and to think of revenge. In your anger you may secretly plan the ultimate retaliation—a life for a life. Recognize that your thoughts are normal as long as you don't act on these impulses. Some people use their anger to lobby for stronger victims' rights, like Mothers Against Drunk Driving (MADD).

My sister was crossing the street with her friends in front of a club. She was hit by a car. He was drunk. He did not have his license or insurance. I am angry with this guy who hit her. Everyone went to the trial but not me. He got five years but it was cut in half. This was his second offense. — Kelvin

My brother was with a group of students outside a bar. The busses from the university were late so the students were waiting for some cabs. He was on the street curb talking. The drunk driver hit my brother first, then a girl, another guy, and a cab. My brother and the girl were killed immediately. The other person survived and is in a wheelchair and the students in the cab survived with minor injuries. My parents went to court. I never went. I never saw the man. I am always angry when I think about the man who did this to my brother. — Mike

I'm mad at the guy who hit her but not mad at my mom for dying. — Krystal

It is important to understand that you have a right to be angry. It is all right to have these feelings. It is also imperative not to take the anger and direct it against yourself by using drugs, alcohol, or injuring yourself in some other way. It is also important not to direct your anger toward others in forms of verbal and physical aggression. The anger needs to be worked through. It is important not to deny your own feelings of anger, but anger should not hurt you or others.

I have mood swings. Sometimes my dad annoys me and I am mad at him for no reason. Some people have perfect lives and I feel jealous. — Meghan

The first couple of Mother's Days, kids talked about their mothers. I was hurt, angry, and felt sorry for myself. — Tasha

I don't really think I have angry feelings. — Karla

I really wasn't that angry. I was upset, not angry. — Krystal

It is important to find a positive way to control feelings of anger. Some people write their thoughts down, as in a poem, diary, journal, or letter. Others need to talk to a professional to help them deal with their anger. At times the professional may feel that ongoing therapy and possibly even medication may be helpful for you. It is also important that you identify the source of these angry feelings and thoughts. It is essential that you learn to cope with anger in a productive way.

When the other kids made Mother's Day cards, I tried to substitute by giving my sister a card. It made me feel better because she was a mother to me. — Tasha

Sometimes I am mad at everything, but it is slowly going away. I want to scream out loud. I want to walk out of the house and never come back. Sometimes I need to go out and sit on the front steps until I cool down. — Meghan

Writing may help teenagers deal with their angry feelings. Some teenagers feel that writing is difficult for them and they would rather talk out their feelings, but writing has the advantage of being personal and private. The written word does not have to be shared with anyone. It is also a way to keep track of your emotional journey. When looking back, you can discover how far you have come in healing. A journal, diary, or scrapbook may be a safe way to get in touch with your deepest emotions. It is also a vehicle to pour out sadness, regrets, loneliness, anger, fears, and feelings of guilt.

Guilt

The loss of a loved one can leave you feeling that your life is out of control. Not being in control over a situation can leave you feeling powerless. Feeling guilty is one way to avoid feeling powerless.

After the death, teenagers remember past events that they shared with the loved one. It is important to understand that we are not all perfect. We say things and feel and do things that we may regret afterward. At times an angry or embarrassing statement may be made impulsively. When the person was alive, you would have been easily forgiven for these outbursts, but of course the person is no longer there to forgive. You are left with feelings of guilt and you have no way to relieve them. There may be feelings of guilt about your own past actions and words, or even the fact that you are alive and your loved one is not. In an attempt to turn back the clock, to undo the wrongs for which they feel guilty, teenagers somehow magically want to restore the loss.

If only I had not teased him, if I was close to him, if I had gone to see what he was doing in the garage.
— Alex

I could have been a lot nicer. I could have put an effort into the relationship. — Kelvin

I wish I had said I love you more often. — Tasha

I remember the stupid things I said and did like in the rebellious stage when I made Dad's life hell.
— Sarah

This year I went to the same university my brother went to. I know I was there to find the guy that killed my brother. I found out he did not live in that place anymore so I dropped out of the university. I felt guilty that I went there in the first place. — Mike

I did not do more things for her, like get her a glass of milk. — Meghan

If only I had delayed her for a few seconds. One thought leads to another . . . if only . . .or what if.
— Krystal

I feel a lot of guilt. I should have listened to his fears about getting away. I did not take my brother with me that day. — Nina

The circumstances under which a person dies does create different emotions in teens. When a loved one has had a prolonged illness, like some cancers, some teenagers feel almost a sense of relief when the person finally dies. Consequently, they may feel guilty for feeling this sense of relief. Children, teenagers, and adults may all feel this way. You may have judged yourself as being selfish for continuing your own life while everyone else may have stopped their lives to care for the sick person. It is a difficult thing to watch a person suffer. Some members of the family may wish for a speedy death to ease the loved one's pain, while others may still be hanging on to the belief that the person is going to take a turn for the better and survive.

It is incredibly difficult to have your life so disrupted by the illness of your loved one, followed by the final disruption, when the loved one dies. Having these feelings of relief does not mean that you do not love your family member. It may simply mean that you are finally free of that particular stress. The sick person will no longer feel his or her own pain. The person will no longer cause you to feel the terrible inner pain that you have been experiencing for a long time.

If your loved one has AIDS (acquired immunodeficiency syndrome), there are still stigmas attached to the illness. Even though people are now more aware and understand AIDS, you may still feel embarrassed. You may feel guilty and not want to be forthcoming in telling people what your loved one is suffering from. You may not want to indicate to others the cause of death when your loved one dies.

There is a great feeling of guilt when a person in the family commits suicide. Could I have prevented it? What if I had been there? Maybe if I had done something. There are too many questions and not enough answers. Sometimes the person has threatened suicide many times and your inner thoughts, in a moment of anger, may have been "go ahead and do it." Suicide leaves the surviving person very vulnerable. You have been taught to appreciate life. You may have religious convictions against suicide. You may think that death comes by sickness or accident, but not by one's own hand. Guilt is a strong emotion that is difficult to relieve. Suicide may bring an onslaught of emotions to the family. It may cause a greater sense of guilt than a natural death.

Another question teenagers may ask themselves is "Am I like them? Am I destined to commit suicide as well?" It is important for you to know that the person who committed suicide is not the same person as you. Suicidal tendencies do not have to run in the family. Suicide is not inherited. You are your own unique person. You may have entirely different coping mechanisms. Your loved one chose suicide as a way to escape inner pain and depression, rather than working through his or her problems. You do not have to choose the same path.

Sudden death, such as that caused by a car accident, can leave survivors feeling guilty because they have had no opportunity to right the wrongs they feel they may have committed before the person's death. Maybe the last thing you said was unkind or maybe you had a fight. Perhaps you feel you never told the loved one that you truly cared. There is no opportunity for closure. One moment the person was there and the next the person was gone.

I remember my sister would ask me if I would go to the mall and I said "no." I remember my grandfather when he was alive wanted to go to lunch and I said "no." The last time I saw my sister before she died, we had a big argument over TV. — Kelvin

Following the death of their loved ones, teenagers may feel guilty for wanting to go out, enjoy themselves, and participate in fun activities. Some teenagers feel that by laughing they are wronging the person who has just died. Are you being disrespectful? Should you be going to parties? Should you be in a constant state of grief? Should you be hiding your feelings altogether?

It is important to recognize that you must give yourself time to grieve, but grieving isn't all of life. It is important that you get on with your own life in an appropriate way. You have probably heard adults say "Your loved one would not want you to grieve so much. Be happy." Happiness does not come automatically. You don't just wake up one day and feel happy. It's a gradual process. There will be reminders of your loved one almost daily. Some people say that it lessens after the first year; some say it takes much longer.

After a year passed, things got better. I had survived without him a year. — Nina

After my sister's death I became more outgoing, less depressed. My sister was very popular. I took a look at my own life and compared it to hers and then started to change. The tragedy changed me for the better. I feel guilty that because of the tragedy I became a better person. — Kelvin

Each person handles grief differently. Some can join in and laugh and others cannot. Some can go to parties and others are not ready. Some hide their emotions and others do not. When your emotions are overpowering, as in a state of depression, then it is important that you have someone to talk with to help you work through your emotions.

You may have troubling feelings about how you are handling your own process of grieving. Sometimes teens are embarrassed by their emotional outbursts, and some teens are embarrassed because they are not feeling the "right" emotions. Teenagers tend to be very hard on themselves.

Maybe if I had only gone to view the open casket, to observe the court case, it might have helped me feel better. — Mike

Depression

My sadness comes and goes. Sometimes I feel I'm living on a roller coaster. Going up and down. Sometimes I am fine and sometimes I'm not. — Karla

When a loved one dies, teens may have difficulty concentrating. They may exhibit a decline in the quality of their schoolwork. They may become withdrawn and isolated from family and friends, and they may seem persistently angry and sad. They may suffer from frequent physical problems and complain about constant fatigue and frequent drowsiness. These are symptoms of depression. Some teenagers may search for ways to fill the void left by the death of a loved one. For teenagers, unresolved grief may be reflected in drug or alcohol abuse, impulsive behavior, and increased inappropriate risk-taking.

Drugs and alcohol cannot help you escape. Alcohol, marijuana, tranquilizers, and sleeping pills are all depressants. This means that you will feel even more depressed when the drug wears off. Cocaine, amphetamines, and other stimulant drugs may make you feel you are on a high, but when the drugs wear off you will feel worse physically and emotionally. Sex used for the wrong reasons can also lead to further pain and depression. You may feel that sex may alleviate the feeling of loneliness and offer some physical comfort. In reality, if you are not ready for a sexual relationship and you are involved for all the wrong reasons, the letdown could shatter your ego. Sex and drugs may allow you to temporarily forget your own pain but they can lead to greater grief. Sex and drugs are roadblocks that prevent you from working through your feelings of loss.

Instead of controlling their moods, teens may find that their moods control them. They may start to feel depressed. Depression is an emotional reaction to loss that includes fears and feelings of sadness, difficulty in concentrating, changes in appetite or sleep patterns, lack of energy, and suicidal thoughts.

I am scared of the dark. I have a lot of fears, like being in parking lots at night. At the beginning I didn't eat. — Nina

At times I get flashbacks. I see my mom in the hospital. She can't breathe. She is gasping for breath. — Meghan

I had some headaches for a while because of stress. — Sarah

I cry to myself in my room. — Kelvin

At night before I fall asleep, I want to cry until morning. — Matthew

Dreams and nightmares may occupy some of your nights. These dreams may be helping you to work through the death of your loved one or through your own feelings of guilt and sadness. Sometimes it is a good idea to write your dreams down. It is also beneficial to write down the emotions the dreams or nightmares release in you. Reading them over and getting in touch with your inner feelings can be very healing.

In my nightmare I see my dad cut up my brother and put him in a suitcase. He tells me and I don't do anything about it. — Nina

It was a dream but I woke up so fast. I was over at the house sleeping with my stepmother. Dad was there and asking if I was sleeping there. If he was

47

really alive, I felt I was taking his place, so I did not know what to answer. Dad then hugged me and I woke up with that warm fuzzy feeling. It was so real.
— Sarah

I had only one dream. My brother was doing his goofy laugh. I could hear it. — Mike

I dream of my sister rarely. A year after her death I dreamt that she was going to die and I had to find her. I was very upset in the dream. My pager went off and I suddenly awoke. I was upset that I couldn't finish the dream because I wanted to tell her things. I dreamt about two months ago that she was not dead. Then I remembered she was not there. I did not want to go to school that day. — Kelvin

I dreamt a week or two after his death. I had a dream that I died. I saw my brother was an angel with God. — Alex

I did have a nightmare at the beginning. I was at school and my mom's best friend picked me up from school and told me my mother had a stroke and died. Maybe it was a way to deal with the death. — Matthew

Sometimes the feeling of depression is so strong that it can affect you both emotionally and physically. Some teenagers have suicidal thoughts. Some are so lethargic that they walk around exhausted and feeling blue. Some feel so emotionally drained that they cannot get out of bed.

Depression may be a way of shutting down the emotional system so that it doesn't suffer a dangerous overload. When emotions shut down the teen can feel nothing.

I was depressed. I usually hang around with friends but I hung around at home doing nothing. My friends were starting to get afraid. They didn't know what to say. It lasted about two months and then I started coming out of it. Once in a while the depression lasts a day or a couple of days and then it goes away. I never felt suicidal. — Alex

It finally hit me. Depression. It was not fair.
— Meghan

I got depressed when I didn't do well on tests.
— Nina

I go in and out of depression. I have had thoughts of suicide recently and a long time ago. I have a lot more pressure on me. I don't like all the pressure.
— Mike

Teenagers suffering from depression can get help through therapy. There are many kinds of professional counseling available to help teens cope with their loss.

Most churches, temples, and synagogues offer help to bereaved teens. Some hospitals and clinics offer bereavement counseling. Schools may have guidance counselors and bereavement counselors. Support groups composed of other individuals dealing with the death of a loved one can be beneficial. Bereavement groups work on helping people to work through their feelings. They offer a setting where others who are in pain can come together. Bereavement groups create a place where a teenager can feel safe. Some teenagers we interviewed felt that individual counseling and support groups were very helpful. Others tried therapy and did not return. Some refused to have any therapy. It is possible that they were not ready for therapy or that they were unable to trust the therapist. When they are ready, they will find a person they trust to talk to.

I went once and did not like feeling forced to talk about it. I felt it was an invasion. Maybe you don't want someone to know how you feel. — Sarah

I have never been to a psychiatrist. I work it out for myself. It works for me. — Mike

I was feeling sad all the time. I was crying one time and the family came up with the idea to see a psychiatrist. I had nothing to lose. It helps. I'm not always as sad. I can get more cheerful. — Matthew

I go to a grieving group. It's helpful to know you are not the only one. — Nina

I started to go to a bereavement group after she died. Talking about it helps. — Kelvin

Religion can sometimes be helpful for teens when dealing with emotional upheavals. Some teens were attracted to their spiritual side and others turned away. A number were angry with God for taking their loved ones away. Some felt comfort in their houses of worship while others were angry or felt little relief in being there. Some teenagers gravitated to religion after the death of a relative and became more religious and others turned away from religion. Some found comfort talking to a minister, priest, or rabbi. A few did not have any religion or a belief in God.

I did not believe in God. I had not gone to church in years. I stopped going when I went to boarding school. We had Christmas celebrations but they were more for family, not religious celebrations. During the funeral, I didn't feel connected to the house of worship. I wish I had. I still do not believe in God but find Buddhism and Rastafarianism interesting. — Mike

The priest was too late to give her last rites. Last rites were very important to the family. The priest said he could do it up to a half hour after death because her soul had not yet left her body. Mom kept saying "Oh my God, she's gone." — Kelvin

The day my mother died, the pastor came over and prayed. At the funeral I was angry at everything. I was angry at God because he took someone away from me. The church is now comforting. I talk to God. I rely on God to take care of her. — Meghan

I pray and go to religious classes. We are Hindu and believe in reincarnation. You live as many lives as you can until you are one with God. When children

die, they only have to live that much more until they are one with God. My brother had two minutes of pain and now he is one with God. — Nina

At the funeral I hated God for taking her away. I did not talk to the pastor. I thought she went to heaven. I thought she was looking out at me. — Tasha

My mom was in so much pain. It was better for her. She is not suffering anymore. God took her. — Matthew

As time passes in the grieving process, it appears that teens gain maturity and wisdom and no longer blame God for the loss. Many rediscover their religions. Many believe that their loved ones have gone to the hereafter. Some believe that their loved ones are watching over them from heaven.

My mother made everyone an angel the Christmas before she died. I think she is an angel watching over us. — Meghan

I see Mom as an angel. — Matthew

I know she is my guardian angel and will protect me in whatever I do. — Tasha

Acceptance

I felt I was at the acceptance stage about a year after her death. — Kelvin

The final stage of grieving is acceptance. Each teenager will reach this point in his or her own time. No two people will reach the stage of acceptance in the same way.

I am not at the stage of acceptance. I don't want to accept. I am so mad and sad. I can't accept it. — Meghan

My mourning for Mom is probably not over. — Krystal

There is no magic awakening from grief. You will not awaken one day to discover that all the pain is gone and the grieving is over. Grieving is a process that takes its time. Teenagers will discover that slowly, ever so slowly, they will awaken to appreciate life around them once more. There will never be a time when you will totally forget your loved one. But time has a way of healing the hurts that are inside of you. Some teenagers feel that having an object to look at or hold will help them keep the memories of their loved ones alive. Some make a shrine with objects and pictures of the loved one. These are some of the ways to feel closer to the deceased. Some need no physical reminders because the loved one remains in their memories and that appears to be enough for them.

How one keeps memories varies from teenager to teenager. Some are content to have pictures and mementos. Others perform rituals like lighting candles and some go to the cemetery to feel closer to their loved ones.

I heard this beautiful story from a family member. She was mourning her grandmother and one day she saw a gold ladybug. It reminded her of her grandmother. It's funny, I now see ladybugs wherever I go. I have Mom's jewelry box, pictures, a necklace, and a pair of her earrings. — Meghan

I took all his Pink Floyd and Grateful Dead CDs. I have his kayak and photographs. Memories are always there. I don't have to keep them or look for them. — Mike

I took her pager chain and giant stuffed animal. Mom lights candles and writes something down at each holiday, in memory of my sister. — Kelvin

I have her wedding band and engagement ring. They were always on her hand. They are symbolic, they were special to her and special to me. I feel closer to her. A picture of her is always in my room. — Tasha

Mom stays there in my head, with the pictures of the good times and bad. I remember her always doing cross-stitching. I have one cross-stitch picture she did in my room. — Matthew

We made a shrine in the den. It has his trophies, his ashes, his paintings, his instruments, and his karate belt. When I miss him I sit in there. — Nina

We have lots of photos. It makes me happy whenever I look at them. I keep the memories in my brain. — Alex

Birthdays and holidays can be a difficult time for bereaved teenagers. Special days bring strong memories rushing back. The memories of the person who has died become especially vivid when a holiday or birthday approaches. Perhaps one of the last memories of the deceased was when the family was together for a holiday or some memorable event, such as a birthday. Some teens feel depressed on the birthday of the deceased. Parents and other siblings may be feeling depressed as well. Sometimes the death occurred on a special day, like your own birthday. In the future, that special day will forever be marked by the remembrance of the death. As time goes by, the pain lessens, but the memories are always with you. On special holidays and birthdays, the memories open up what you thought were closed wounds and you may start to feel pain again.

The anniversary of a death can also be very painful. In traditional Jewish homes, a *yahrzeit* candle (yahr = year, zeit

= time) is lit every year to mark the anniversary of the death and to honor the remembrance of the one who died. Within the first year after the death, there is an unveiling, which is a special Jewish ceremony to dedicate the headstone placed at the person's grave. Many people feel especially sad at the anniversary of a death even though they may not feel much grief at other times of the year. Many people conduct their own rituals to remember the death of a loved one. They may write a poem or a letter, place flowers on the grave site, or get together with people who knew the loved one and reminisce about the good times.

Special days are difficult because those are the days you are supposed to be feeling joy and happiness. Again, how does one enjoy the season of Christmas or a birthday party when the loved one is no longer present to share in the event? If a teenager had a father or mother who died, Mother's Day and Father's Day can be difficult for them. On this special day they cannot hide their feelings. They feel all alone without their loved ones.

I sit and think of her, the happy times, holidays, thinking of her charismatic personality. She liked to cook. Christmas dinners were special. The first couple of Mother's Days and holidays were hard. At school when kids talked about Mother's Day, it hurt and I felt sorry for myself. — Tasha

On her birthday the priest came over and we had Mass in the backyard. — Kelvin

I reflect on birthdays. — Mike

It is important to know that anniversaries are usually hard on everyone who survives a death. This may be the time for you to find something special to do for yourself. It might mean going for a walk, a quiet moment with a friend, or a time to look at pictures and recall memories of your loved one. It is important for you to allow yourself to grieve again.

The cemetery can prove to be a source of comfort to the bereaved teenager. Some find the cemetery a spiritual place, but others do not feel comfortable at the cemetery. At times teenagers go to the cemetery to feel closer to their loved ones. As time heals, some teens feel that the need to go to the cemetery becomes less urgent.

When I visit, I feel sad, but I feel closer to Mom. The body is right under me. I am closer to her. — Matthew

I hate going to cemeteries and hospitals. I have to go but I dislike it. — Meghan

The family goes to the cemetery often. I don't feel that the cemetery does anything for me. — Tasha

I went a lot at the beginning, almost every week-end. When I feel upset, I go to the cemetery and I feel better. — Kelvin

Many of the teenagers we interviewed felt the presence of their loved ones after their deaths. It may have been through dreams or just an uncanny feeling that the spirit of the person was there. Some saw the presence as comforting and others felt it was a warning. Some felt that the loved one was trying to communicate with them. The presence offered a much needed emotional connection.

I scored my first goal and felt she was there. I visited her grave on Mother's Day. I felt sad. I felt that she was telling me not to cry. — Meghan

I see her as an angel protecting me. I didn't go out with friends one night. I felt she did not want me to go. Someone was shot that night. On one other night I felt Mom protected me. There were fights and people got trampled. I felt Mom held me back from going. — Tasha

A month after his death, it was a full moon and the locks in the van started to go up and down real fast. When I am feeling a certain way, a song will come on over the radio. I will ask my brother a question and a song will come on and answer me. My brother is always in the back of my mind. I feel he is still around. I talk to him. — Nina

When I saw her body, I felt she was there in my brain. It was both comforting and frightening. On a couple of occasions I felt she was there. — Matthew

Meghan and Matthew tell the story of a little boy their mom had taught. The boy, Andrew, was greatly affected by losing one of his favorite teachers. He wrote the following poem and entered it into a contest. He won the contest and then sent the poem to the *Oprah Winfrey Show*. The topic of the show was "Teachers Who Made an Impact on Children's Lives."

> I remember your beautiful face,
> the beauty that illness could not erase.
> I remember your smile and gentle touch,
> the way you taught me so very much.
> The dinosaur exhibit, the park and zoo,
> all of these hold memories of you.
> I got so angry when I heard that day,
> Why had God taken you away?
> It took a while for me to see,
> what the answer could ever be.
> The answer became as clear as glass,
> God needed you there to teach his class.
> So good-bye sweet teacher, you taught me well,
> Angel School is starting, God's
> ringing the bell.

The family, including Andrew, was invited to appear on the *Oprah Winfrey Show*. The poem was read, a plaque was presented, and a slide show was shown with pictures of Meghan and Matthew's mom.

At the beginning of the show I was fine. Then it hit me when the poem was read. I was crying and felt sad. It was a good thing for Mom. — Matthew

There were the newspapers, the Oprah Winfrey Show, *it just keeps on going. Keeping memories, you*

want it to stop hurting. It never will stop hurting.
— Meghan

This was a public occasion watched by millions of viewers. Most tributes to the dead are low-key and designed for the individual or the immediate family. Some place their tributes or memorials in the newspaper. Some continue this practice yearly. They place poems and statements in newspapers annually to mark the anniversary of the death of a loved one. Some also include a picture of the deceased in happier times. It is a public way of sharing one's grief.

Some teenagers feel that memories of the loved one will fade over time. They get anxious when they say that they cannot remember a loved one's laugh or face. Many do not want these precious memories to die away just as the loved one has died away.

Things started to get fuzzy and I did not want things to get fuzzy. I bought a book filled with captions like "Today I am feeling . . . " and "At Christmas time without him I feel. . . ." I kept up the book for a little while. I wanted to remember, and by reading what I wrote it helps me to remember. — Sarah

My aunt is open and loving. She tries to bring Mom to us by helping to keep the memories. My aunt gives us things that are angels, like our mom, the angel.
— Meghan

Some teenagers try to make sense of the death that occurred. They are searching for answers. It is especially difficult when the person who died was a young child. How does one make sense of a young child dying? Nina tells a beautiful tale of the Lord of Ganesh.

A woman was taking a bath. She needed some one to protect her because her husband was out, so she made a statue out of clay. It was brought to life. She said to the boy, "You are my son, do not let anyone pass through this door." The husband came home and said to the boy, "Let me pass through this door." The little boy said, "No." He was protecting his mom. In a rage of anger, the father cut off the boy's head. That is why Lord Ganesh has an elephant's head symbolizing the god of getting through obstacles. The story is symbolic to me because my little brother protected Mom and that is how he died. Just like Ganesh, my brother was chubby. Ganesh has four hands and in one there is something sweet. My brother always ate a sweet called laddu. Ganesh has a mouse on his feet. Two days before my brother's death there was a mouse in my room. My brother always prayed to Ganesh, one of several gods in Hinduism. He sacrificed himself for us. — Nina

The final part of the acceptance stage is looking back and remembering the lessons taught by the loved one. As time goes by, his or her words and values become a part of your existence. You may not agree with these ideas and how this person handled his or her life, but you learn to appreciate all that the deceased has done for you.

Everything she taught me has come back. God has provided me with a great family. I am grateful for what I have. — Tasha

It is most difficult to watch the family grow away from the loved one who died. Parents may start to date and find another partner. It is difficult to accept this situation, but everyone has to move on with their lives.

Dad has a girlfriend. I did not like her at first. Adults need a companion. It doesn't have to replace my love for Mom. Dad always loved Mom. Still it's sad, but he needed companionship. — Tasha

The grieving process is a difficult process to go through for everyone. There are many stages and detours along the way until you finally accept the loss of your loved one. If you have difficulty getting there on your own, professional help is available.

Recovery

People working with teenagers who have suffered a death in the family feel that resolving a significant loss may take years rather than months. Grieving is a process that occurs slowly over time. Researchers find that the intensity of grief remains constant for a greater time period than people anticipate or expect. Some professionals like to advise teenagers that the grieving period does not just stop suddenly and that it is a gradual and individual process. Your friends, who mean well, may feel that you have done enough grieving. Your year is up and you should be back to feeling "normal" again. They are not you. They don't understand that there is no time limit to grieving. The clock continues to tick.

> There is a great deal of pain in life
> and perhaps the only pain that can be
> avoided is the pain that comes from
> trying to avoid pain.
> —R. D. Laing

A manual put out by the Tragic Events Support Team of a local Toronto school district creates the image of a "Wall of Pain," a barrier that teenagers have to pass through in order to risk loving someone again. This wall can have different dimensions. It can have an area where teenagers get stuck in their grief and cannot rid themselves of their pain. There is the area where teenagers work through their pain by developing an understanding of what their loved one meant to them. There is also the area where teenagers are overwhelmed by their pain and are unable to acknowledge it. An expert in the grieving process can help teenagers get through this wall.

The therapeutic process can be helpful to teenagers because they can work with a person who is an understanding helper. This person is there to guide them through their grieving process. If at any time teens feel that they are strong enough to handle their own grief, they can terminate the sessions. They then feel that they have taken control of their lives. Teenagers can benefit from the guidance of a professional at any stage in their grieving process. It could be before the death even occurs, right at the funeral, immediately afterward, or even years later when they are adults. A teenager might need special help when dealing with emotions such as anger or depression. Some teens bury their grief so deep that as adults they need the guidance of a therapist to walk them back in time to relive their suppressed emotions. The therapist is there to help in understanding and interpreting these emotions.

Factors that are associated with the death of a loved one may require the intervention of a trained therapist. The manner of a loved one's death may not be easily accepted by the teenager, and he or she may need help in the healing process. Unanticipated deaths as a result of drunk driving, accidents, murder, or suicide are deaths that teenagers are not prepared for and may not be able to cope with on their own. Even anticipated deaths from long-term illnesses may be very hard for teenagers to cope with after the loved one has finally died. If the deceased in life was physically, sexually, or verbally abusive, teenagers may be feeling mixed emotions about the death. Should they hate the person, or should they feel relieved? Why do they still feel pain instead of relief when a hurtful person has finally left their lives for good? Teenagers may need some counseling to work through their conflicting emotions.

Some teenagers feel comfortable if they can express their feelings to someone such as a family member or a friend. Some teenagers feel that they can handle their own problems. Some have a strong network of family and friends who can help them through the grieving process. Others may need the help of a professional so that their feelings are heard and understood by an outsider and they don't have to feel that they are being judged. The therapeutic process with a psychologist, social worker, psychotherapist, psychiatrist, or clergyman is a confidential one and teens can feel safe in this kind of relationship.

Therapists have different types of training, backgrounds, and philosophies. All have been trained to listen to you and help you on the road to recovery. You can speak to your family doctor or clergyman to get the name of a therapist or at least some advice on where to look. Your clergyman has been trained in bereavement counseling and this might be a good place to begin. In school there may be guidance counselors, social workers, or psychologists who can assist you. They may be able to refer you to someone who understands the dynamics of teenagers who are coping with bereavement. There are individual therapists and there are family therapists. At times having the family in a session all together can be helpful. At other times you may want to deal with your personal feelings without other family members present. You might consider asking your friends for advice. Perhaps they themselves have been part of a teenage bereavement group that they can recommend to you. They may know a counselor who can help. You can ask an adult you trust. It would be beneficial to talk to your parents so that they can support your decision to seek help through counseling. Depending on the country or city where you live, there may be a charge for therapy. Your family members will know if there is money in the budget or a medical plan to cover the expenses of a therapist. Some bereavement groups do not charge for their services.

It is important to understand that seeking help from an expert is your choice and that the help gained may make your life a little bit easier. But if you find that you are not comfortable with the therapeutic relationship, try another therapist. You are not committed to this relationship if you are feeling great discomfort. You may be glad that you changed. Therapy can bring to the surface many emotions that you have tried to hide. It is all right to allow them to come to the surface in the therapist's office. It is all right to feel.

We have interviewed ministers, rabbis, psychotherapists, and social workers to find out how they have helped teenagers work through the grieving process. Although they maintain that each teenager is unique, they do have some techniques that appear to be beneficial for most teens.

Therapists and Clergy Speak Out

Although therapists and clergy have different methodologies, one thing is paramount—they care. Bereavement counselors, whether they are therapists or clergy, have been trained to listen. Some will be more interactive. Some will be direct in their questioning styles. Some will be indirect and try to lead you to your own answers. Together, both of you will work toward the common goal of helping you work through your loss.

> I see grieving as a process in which teenagers come into psychotherapy looking for a more effective way to deal with their impending reality. I first look at what the teenager's level of acceptance is. Then based on the level of insight and acceptance I explore with the teenager what he or she hopes to get out of psychotherapy. Most people say that they need a place where they feel comfortable enough to express their feelings and thoughts without being judged. Above all I help them to deal with a myriad of feelings that assault them daily. — Social worker

> It is important that teenagers trust the therapist right from the beginning. Are they here because they want to be or did someone drag them in? It is important that they want to be here. I want them to know that it is a safe place, that I respect their opinions, and that if they think it may not be helpful now, they can come back at any time. — Psychologist

The first session a teenager has with a therapist includes information gathering. The teenager will be feeling out the situation to see if he or she is comfortable in the session. The teen may look at the bereavement counselor and ask himself or herself a number of questions. Does this person appear to be trustworthy? Can I talk to this person? Do I feel that this professional can help me? Am I feeling good about being here in this room? This is also a time to ask the therapist questions. What are some of your techniques? What are your expectations of me? Do you need the rest of my family to be involved in the therapy? There are, of course, two questions that are much more difficult for the therapist to answer. How long do I have to come here? When will the hurting stop? Truthfully, the therapist doesn't know the answers to the last two questions. What you say in therapy stays between you and the bereavement counselor. It is totally confidential.

Do You Counsel Before Death Occurs?

Counseling can occur at any time. Sometimes counseling is suggested before the loved one dies. It may be helpful to try to put things into perspective emotionally and spiritually before a loss. Many times when a loved one is sick and at home, the rest of the family doesn't have time to communicate with each other. Many times a teenager will be feeling emotionally abandoned. The reality is just too difficult to face and there doesn't appear to be anyone who has the time to help. These teens are isolated in their own world of sadness. Counseling or talking to a member of the clergy may be helpful to the emotionally drained teenager.

I see counseling before a death occurs as a more recent thing. People are becoming more aware of the needs of children and teenagers. — Psychologist

Teenagers need to talk about what they want to talk about. They don't want to think about the impending death. Sometimes it is hard for kids to process what is really going on. They may not want to deal with it before the death. — Minister

I have worked with teenagers dying from AIDS. I had to help one teenager work through his anger at himself for knowingly engaging in high risk behavior. His behavior and anger were affecting the family. I had to help the family deal with the changing dynamics. — Social worker

Teenagers may not be at the stage where they will accept counseling before the death occurs. They may not be able to acknowledge out loud that the loved one is dying. They may still be feeling hopeful or have feelings of denial. This is the time that professionals may see the whole family to discuss how much the teenager should be involved with the full process of the death. Should he or she attend the funeral? If the teenager attends, should he or she take part in the rituals?

The families come in with concerns, such as should their child go to the funeral or how does one prepare a teenager for the death of a mother. One mother was writing a book to help her teenagers get

through the milestones in their lives without her. One part discussed what to do when her daughter was going to get her period. — Psychologist

Some families want to discuss the prefuneral arrangements. Some teenagers just want to know, "If my mom dies, where is she going?" — Minister

With a sudden death there is no opportunity for counseling or preparation beforehand. The loved one dies suddenly and the surrounding family members are left in shock.

The Initial Stages of Grief

One of the first stages the teenager will experience after the death of a loved one is a feeling of shock. Initially, teenagers feel so emotionally overwhelmed that talking to anybody is a burden. They need to absorb the news internally.

A member of the family may have already telephoned a cleric, who may be present at the death of the loved one. The cleric may have been the first person from outside the family who will ask to speak to you. Members of the clergy usually try to make the initial stage of grief comfortable for all family members. There is an understanding that the whole family is under severe stress.

When the loved one has died, I meet with the family and speak with them at length. If I am preparing the eulogy, I ask everyone present to participate. I ask the teenagers to share their irreplaceable anecdotes. Some

70

teenagers are so knotted up that this is a difficult task for them. To get them to share their stories, I might ask them some pointed questions. Tell me of a special memory when you think of your loved one. Did your loved one ever give you a special gift that is in your bedroom? Did your loved one ever do something that particularly reminds you of him or her? Did you ever go someplace together, a special place just for the two of you? — Rabbi

Many teenagers grow up without adult influence. In our church, adults connect with youth on the youth's turf. In the initial stage of loss, the pastor may be the first adult they connect with. The adult will listen, be sincere, be confidential, and allow the teenager to feel safe. Sometimes peers are not enough. — Minister

In the early stages of bereavement, many teenagers are being very protective of parents and siblings and are not at the stage where therapy may be effective. — Psychologist

Although the whole family is feeling shock, family members have to get themselves prepared for the funeral. Even before attending, there may be monumental tasks, such as picking out caskets and making telephone calls to friends, relatives, and business associates. A notice in the newspaper may have to be called in. The lawyer may have to be contacted to see if a will had been prepared. In a few situations, the actual funeral arrangements may become the teenager's responsibility. As well as dealing with his or her own grief, the teenager is surrounded by others who may not be functioning at their best.

During the funeral it is important for teenagers to be able to say their good-byes. All therapists and clergy that we interviewed felt that attendance at the funeral was very important. Some professionals feel that taking part in the ceremony is also important for teenagers. It will be a memory that will remain with them forever. Some teenagers will take part in the service and others will not feel emotionally ready to do so.

> *I strongly encourage teenagers to attend the funeral as a way of helping them to confront the reality of the passing of a loved one. Equally important is the public sharing of emotions, such as occurs during a wake or shiva, as well as the private time that teenagers needs to mourn.* — Social worker

> *I invite the children or teenagers to compose a letter and place it in an envelope in the coffin. This letter could be inserted anytime before burial. It could also be a picture. I emphasize that they make a copy to look at when they want to reminisce. I ask them if they would like to do a reading, a poem, or some farewell at the funeral or at the grave site. Some are not comfortable with this. Sometimes just dropping a flower on the coffin at the burial helps to say good-bye.* — Rabbi

After the death of a loved one, some teenagers will need the comfort of talking. Others will gravitate to songs, videos, chat lines on the Internet, books, psalms, and poems. Teens will try to make sense of what has just happened to them. They may be searching for others who have felt the same pain. They may be looking for resources that can help them find answers and an understanding of what has happened. The following is a psalm that sometimes helps and is read at a number of funerals.

> To every thing there is a season,
> and a time to every purpose
> under heaven.
> A time to be born, and a time to die;
> a time to plant, and a time to
> pluck up that which is planted;
> A time to kill, and a time to heal;
> a time to break down,
> and a time to build up;
> A time to weep, and a time to laugh;
> a time to mourn, and a time to dance;
> A time to cast away stones,
> and a time to gather stones together;
> A time to embrace,
> and a time to refrain from embracing;
> A time to get, and a time to lose;
> a time to keep, and a time to cast away;
> A time to rend, and a time to sew;
> a time to keep silence,
> and a time to speak;
> A time to love, and a time to hate;
> a time of war,
> and a time of peace.
>
> 4 Ecclesiastes 3:1

Some families ask their clergy if teenagers should be pallbearers. This means holding and transporting the casket to the burial site. It is important that teenagers identify their needs and be allowed to participate in the funeral service or have the opportunity to say that they don't wish to participate. In Judaism, members of the immediate family wear a ribbon and sit shiva. Although grandchildren do not normally sit shiva or wear a ribbon, sometimes they are allowed to emulate their parents in order to handle their grief. Teenagers may not be in any condition to participate in the funeral, or they may be waiting for an opportunity to take part, if you let them.

> *Sometimes I have poems ready to hand out to the teenager if I feel he or she can handle it. One time I was at the grave site of a father who had died. The son was rebellious and would not talk. I said that I would love it if he would say something and I handed him a poem that began "I was a rebellious son . . ."* He read it and was finally able to cry. I tend to try to anticipate possibilities and hand teenagers a way in. — Rabbi

In Littleton, Colorado, on April 20, 1999, twelve teenagers and one teacher were murdered by two teenage boys, who then committed suicide. The event left millions of people around the world in shock. Many did not know how to handle their grief and pain. As the events were broadcast on the television and reported in the newspapers, people around the world watched and shared in the mourning. At the memorial services, poems and letters were read, songs were sung, and when each of the murdered teens' names

74

was read, a dove was released into the air. Counselors came from all over the United States to help the surviving teenagers and their families.

In Taber, Alberta, another tragedy struck right after the killings in Colorado. A fourteen-year-old boy went into his school and shot dead one teenager and seriously injured another. "The community is in a state of shock and will probably stay that way for the next few days," Mayor Phillips reported. Groups of students quietly left flowers in the wet, blowing snow. At the school's main door, a handwritten note was pinned to a bouquet of red roses. "You will never be forgotten," it read.

Going into a state of shock is a way for the mind to close down and protect the emotional integrity of the sufferer. The teenager has been hit hard by the news that someone he or she cared about has died. The teen goes into a state of shock, or emotional numbness. When the shock lessens, the person attempts to deal with the reality of the death. Sometimes the shock is so great, however, that the person goes into a state of denial. They may be thinking, "This could not possibly be happening to me. This is a dream. If I go to sleep and wake up, it will be like yesterday and then everything will be all right again."

Basically I want the teenagers to know that shock and denial are to be expected and there is nothing wrong in feeling this way. — Psychotherapist

They want a quick fix. They want the pain to go away. When I counsel, I may take them through the funeral again. We discuss images that haunt them.

We talk about whether the casket was open or closed. My focus is on whether they were glad they went, whether their friends came, what happened to the body, whether or not they found comfort, and how they keep the loved one's presence alive.
— Psychologist

Many teenagers say that they could not remember the events of the funeral as they were in deep shock. Years later, with the help of a therapist, they begin to remember and the healing begins. Many remember which of their friends supported them at the funeral. Looking around at all the faces at the funeral and finding their friends was very helpful to them in their initial stages of grieving.

Changing Emotions
After a Death

All therapists and clergy we interviewed felt that teenagers needed friends during a period of loss and grieving. Friends can be supportive at any stage after the death of a loved one, from the first realization of loss to the funeral, and to the stages thereafter. Friends offer a much needed support network. Sometimes friends and family members were just not enough or did not have the answers teens were seeking, and therapists and clergy helped fill in the gaps.

I encourage teenagers to seek the company of their friends. Mourning can be a very lonely experience because the meaning of the loss is personal to you. But friends can help take the aloneness away by supporting you in your grief. What I am trying to say is that grieving may be a lonely process but it does not have to be handled alone. You may not feel like going out and having fun with them, but it is important to remember that friends are there for you. Good friends provide comfort, support, and understanding.
— Social worker

Friends can be helpful as informal bereavement groups. I went to visit a teenager who was grieving. He had two friends in the room with him. Together as a group we talked about our losses. It was a friendly environment. Friends can provide some comfort and can learn and share how you feel. — Rabbi

Friends are important just because they are there. They are there to listen to the same story over and over again. Sometimes friends are there just to be silent and not offer stupid remarks or ask for anything in return. A friend can be patient and allow someone to grieve at his or her own pace. The therapist, the clergyman, and the family members can also serve in this role.

Family Members

Everybody in the family is mourning in their own way. Some teenagers may isolate themselves, some may gravitate to their friends, and others may seek out other family members. Some may be open with their feelings, and others may close down. Families mourn together but individuals mourn alone.

When the parent dies, I deal with the fears and the vulnerability of the teenager. I also deal with the blame, the self-blame, the guilt, the unfinished business. Much depends on the circumstances surrounding how the parent dies. For the most part teenagers go through different stages of feelings. When a sibling dies, it strikes at the teenager's sense of immortality. Teenagers grapple with questions such as "Why my mom?" or "Why my sister?" I encourage teenagers to share their thoughts and feelings with the other family members. I ask them to find a medium for them to express their feelings, to draw, to paint, to write a poem, keep a journal, to dance, to be open to their dreams. Dreams are a way for the unconscious to come to the forefront. — Social worker

You may not be able to deal with the new family dynamics. You may be left as the only child or you may be left without your mother or father. Your role in the family will be new. You may not like it at first, but in time the reality will set in and you come to accept the new situation. In therapy, you may be able to talk about how it used to be and how it is now. At home it may be difficult to bring up the past, but in therapy it is desirable to bring up past memories. With the help of the bereavement counselor you will get impartial feedback. You may need a shoulder to cry on or just someone to tell you that what you are feeling is normal. Sometimes, although you may love your family members, you don't want to share your most intimate and sometimes confusing thoughts. With the counselor you can express yourself freely and get help in dealing with your emotions.

Anger and Guilt

Anger is a very powerful emotion. Some teenagers are afraid of expressing their anger. Some teenagers are disturbed about even having angry feelings toward the person who died. They don't think that this is right, and they judge themselves for feeling anger. But anger is a healthy emotion when it is understood as being an essential part of the grieving process.

In my sessions, I encourage teenagers to verbalize their anger as a way to get to the hurt and pain that is underneath it. Therapy offers a safe place for them to do this. Some people stay stuck in their anger for a long time. It is important to help them realize that there is something beyond the anger. I encourage and support teenagers to pick up pillows and punch them if they need to. — Social worker

Anger may be appropriate. We may want to find out who the teenager is really angry at. Sometimes it is good to voice it, to identify the sources. Sometimes joining a group such as MADD (Mothers Against Drunk Driving) is helpful. Keeping a journal or writing or listening to music may be helpful, or doing something to release the stress, such as exercising. Teenagers must make the decision that they are not going to let anger eat them alive. It is important to see there are good things happening in this world. — Psychologist

I ask questions. The teenagers say "I am really mad." I reply back with "You are mad because. . . ." Together we work on pinpointing what they are angry about. It helps with their pain and allows them to focus on change. — Minister

Sometimes I encourage the teenagers to keep a diary, a memory book, or a photo book. — Rabbi

At times teenagers are angry at God, especially at the beginning of the grieving process. Is God to be held accountable for the death of the loved one? Teenagers may wonder, if God is good, kind, and loving, why then was their loved one taken away?

I talk with teenagers about my own experience with the death of a loved one. When it happened, I yelled, "It's not fair." Sometimes teenagers want God to make them more powerful. Sometimes teenagers see God as being like a parent who makes everything all right, rather than understanding the inevitability of death. God is not responsible for accidents. Don't associate God with every fallen life. — Rabbi

God is Love. God works for good. It does not mean that bad things do not happen. — Minister

Many teenagers feel some anger. Some internalize it and others act on it. Anger may be helpful, but when it gets out of hand the teenager will need some assistance in coping with these feelings.

Howard Knoff, past president of the U.S. National Association of School Psychologists and a professor of school psychology, was reported to say that the focus in the Littleton, Colorado, murders was taking a new form, because the United States was leaving the disbelief stage of its collective understanding of the killings and was entering the anger stage. This means that people were looking for someone to blame, in this case the parents of the killers. Many times teenagers and adults want to put the blame on others. Many times they also put the blame on themselves. Sometimes anger and guilt go hand in hand.

A sense of guilt or remorse is common. For some teenagers this can be very crippling. Along with depression, it can immobilize the person. Guilt is a form of self-punishment for things that the teen believes should have happened, could have happened, or did happen. Guilt means dealing with regrets, with what could have been but now can never be. The loved one has now died, and the teenager cannot alter that fact.

I get the person to express what the guilt is and explore the irrationality of the guilt with the person. I explore the ideas behind the guilt. Most guilt is irrationally based. — Psychotherapist

Some teenagers take on guilt for the death of their loved ones. They may have seen themselves as omnipotent. But when the death of a loved one occurs, they are unable to will someone back to life. — Rabbi

Guilt is very individualistic. I work with the teenager on terminology. The teenager says "I killed my brother." Together we look at rational and irrational feelings. I look at factual information. The teenager reports "I was playing outside. I was supposed to watch him. I called out. He got run over." The teenager feels responsible for the death of his brother. Another example: "I was at the scene of the accident. I should have done something to save his life. I should have done CPR." Sometimes as a therapist I need to get the police report and the coroner's report to help the teenager with his or her feelings of guilt. There is also the sibling survivor's guilt. When a sibling dies and the surviving child is the only one left, the child hears his or her parents grieve so much for the child that died that the surviving child sometimes feels "Did the wrong kid die? If I died would my parents be OK?" — Psychologist

I suggest that the teenager write a letter to the person who died. Mailing it is a symbolic way of giving it to the person. Writing is very important. Teenagers can pour out their hearts. They can start the healing process and forgive themselves. — Minister

When a loved one commits suicide, the feelings of guilt can be very strong in the surviving members of the family. They have many questions and no one is there to give them answers or relieve their feelings of guilt. Sometimes there is no suicide note and the family is left in the dark. At other times there is a suicide note that either puts blame on the family or asks the family for forgiveness. One will always ask oneself, did I do enough? There is no easy way to handle the suicide of a loved one.

I help the teenager understand that the choice of suicide was ultimately the responsibility of the loved one. Guilt comes in the form of "I should have been aware that the person was feeling this way. If only I had known, I could have stopped it from happening." The sad fact is that no one can stop someone who is determined to commit suicide. We can urge a person to seek professional help. We can, as family members and friends, be supportive and understanding, but in the final analysis a person who is determined to commit suicide will do it, regardless of our best intentions or interventions. — Social worker

The following list gives an idea of some of the special features of suicide.

- Suicide attempts can often be seen as a call for help.

- Suicide is often an attempt to communicate extreme unhappiness.

- Suicide often immediately follows a crisis, which is a time of intense emotional turmoil when a person's coping abilities are overwhelmed.

- Often the person desiring suicide has many accumulated disappointments that have gone unresolved and are hidden deep within. The latest event is simply the last straw.

- Most people who think about killing themselves give clues or warnings. They are asking for help.

- In many cases suicide can be prevented. There are ways to help.

- Sometimes, no matter what someone does to help, the person may attempt or complete the act.

- Suicide is complex. There is no single cause.

Dr. Robert Stevenson has provided some guidelines to help those who have had a suicide in the family.

- Assist the bereaved to clarify their thoughts and feelings.

- Put an end to unfounded rumors that cause unnecessary additional pain.

- Don't romanticize the suicide by saying that the person is "better off."

- Help the bereaved by recalling the complete person with human strengths and weaknesses.

If you are the relative of a suicide victim it is important for you to understand that the therapist is listening compassionately to your story. The therapist is not there to make any moral judgments about the deceased or the person's final act. It is imperative that you as the survivor work through your own beliefs and attitudes toward suicide. It is vital that you get past the final moments of the suicide and keep in your heart and soul the loved one's life. You and your family might consider joining a support group for relatives of suicide victims to help in the healing process.

Many teenagers feel guilty because they cannot forgive the person who was responsible for the death of their loved ones. They feel that they will never forgive the drunk driver who killed a sibling or the murderer who gunned down a loved one. Many teenagers feel that they should be forgiving but just can't. Others know that they will never forgive, and still others turn to religion to help them through the process of forgiving.

Who is the big loser if you don't forgive? Anger is an emotional cancer. Bitterness is in store for those who do not forgive. — Minister

The person who has done the act must own up to what he or she has done wrong. Then forgiveness can come. — Rabbi

Many teenagers feel some sense of guilt after a loved one has died. When a person cannot get past feelings of guilt and anger and gets stuck in this emotional state, it is a good time to seek help from a counselor. The therapist will work with the teenager to help him or her see the situation more clearly.

Depression

Often when teenagers lose someone close to them, they become very sad and remorseful. Depression is a natural response to loss. It is a sign of how important the person was to the teenager. When depressed, people may withdraw into themselves and away from the world. Their sleep patterns may change and they may gain or lose weight. They may feel listless or tired a lot of the time, and their concentration may be poor. They may go through a period where they lose interest in school and friends. Finally, they feel unhappy most of the time.

Psychotherapeutically, it is important to help teenagers mourn their loss in an appropriate manner. Depression can also become anger turned inwards toward the self. It is therefore important to help teenagers verbalize their feelings of loss. There can be a role for antidepressant medication if needed.
— Psychotherapist

Depressed—why shouldn't you be, given the loss. In therapy we work on peeling away the layers. I may pose questions such as "What is the hardest time?" There may be fears such as "I won't remember what she looks like" or "I am never going to see them again." I may have to do behavior-cognitive therapy and make teenagers relive the death. I may do some systematic desensitizations, that is, slowly desensitizing them to their fears. I may ask them to practice progressive relaxation with special breathing techniques. If the teenager is suicidal, I must take action. My main job is to keep the teenager safe. — Psychologist

I listen to teenagers' fears. I may refer them for therapy. Managed medication may be vital, but there is no quick solution. — Rabbi

I will refer teens to professional counselors. I also offer small group support. People share their struggles and people pray together. It is a safe and structured environment where people talk, and together everyone listens. — Minister

Sometimes the memories of the death of your loved one are so vivid in your mind that you feel stressed out.

Post-traumatic stress can take many forms: nightmares, pictures in your mind of your loved one's death, fear that someone else close to you will die, and painful sadness. Post-traumatic stress can be experienced whenever something reminds you of your loved one. It could be a shared song, being in a certain place, a smell, or seeing someone that reminds you of your loved one. Sometimes you can get physical symptoms such as anxiety, heart palpitations, and panic attacks. When feeling over-whelmed, you might just try calling a friend, going for a walk, watching a video, going to see a movie, doing deep relaxation exercises, meditating, or doing yoga. When the pain becomes unbearable or you feel you are stuck in a rut and cannot get out, remember that therapists and clergy are there to help you.

Acceptance

Acceptance is the realization that the final outcome could not have been different regardless of what one said or did, regardless of one's best intentions or aspirations. Acceptance is the result of knowing on both an emotional and an intellectual level that the dead person is not going to come back to life, that the loss of the loved one is for-ever. Acceptance does not mean that you don't miss the person or feel sad that the person is no longer alive. It means that you are grateful for that person having shared his or her life with you.

I encourage a remembrance throughout the process. For some people, when they get to the acceptance stage, they do not need an external reminder because the memories of the deceased are inside them. Others may want an external memorial to the loved one in the form of pictures or mementos. — Psychotherapist

It is important to talk freely about death. Unhappy things need to be confronted. — Minister

Mementos help in the nostalgia, the longing for the deceased person. Writing down your thoughts and feelings is good therapy. — Rabbi

This is the time for putting the loved one in a particular place, always a part of you, in your heart. You might talk to the person in your head, or you may carry a memento with you at all times. Whatever works for you. At times, developing rituals is important for the teenagers, but the rituals should be significant for them. I remember a group of teenagers who got together with their guitars at the accident site where their friend died. They played music and talked. This was more meaningful to them and helpful in handling their grief. It is important for teenagers to be creative and find their own rituals to help them in the healing process. — Psychologist

When you get to the acceptance stage, you will feel that you can handle your life better psychologically and emotionally. This is the time that the therapist will terminate your sessions, as you are now better able to handle your grief independently. If you ever need to have a helping hand again, you know that you are always welcome to go back to a therapist.

Coping with Loss

Many therapists and clergy use special verbal and visual techniques to help teenagers to open up and work through their feelings. Many of the teenagers interviewed used these techniques to help them through the grieving period. Some kept journals; others wrote poetry. Some used colored circles to depict their emotions. Whatever techniques are used, the test of their value is whether or not they help.

> *I ask teenagers to visualize their loved ones and conduct a dialogue with them. It helps for teenagers to forgive the loved one for dying and to forgive themselves for feeling the way they do about the loved one. I ask them to draw pictures of their emotions and feelings, to bring in pictures of the loved one or an object that symbolizes the person.* — Social worker

> *I remember putting out two figurines and letting the person act out. It was helpful to understand the person's fears. Sometimes we talk about the relationship to figures in the Bible and how they pertain to the teenager's life today.* — Rabbi

> *At times I ask teenagers to bring in music that they enjoy. Sometimes they bring in poetry or write stories that they are willing to share. Sometimes they*

are creative in an area of dance. I remember a teen-ager whose father had died. She did a dance to Barbara Streisand's "Papa Can You Hear Me?" It was helpful in expressing her grief. When teenagers are angry, at times I ask them to tape-record their yelling and screaming and swearing. I don't want them to edit it. I just want them to get it out. It helps to pick away at the layers of the onion to find the sources of the anger or discontent. When working with bereavement groups, I use a number of games and techniques. — Psychologist

The Question Box

In a bereavement group different techniques are used to help get individuals to open up with each other and share their thoughts, experiences, and emotions. One technique is the "question box." Each member of the group is given a piece of paper and asked to write any question on a topic chosen by the bereavement group leader. For exam-ple, the topic could be on feeling guilty. The box is then passed around and each person places his or her question in the box. Each member then takes a turn reading one question from the box. Of course, the writers of the ques-tions remain anonymous. There is a discussion on each question pulled from the box. At times a technique like this is helpful because teenagers don't have to risk sharing their personal concerns openly in a forum where they have yet to develop a feeling of trust. As the group dynam-ics change and the bereavement group becomes a place where people feel safe and trusting, questions can then be asked freely by identifiable individuals.

The Weather Inside

This technique is used for younger children but sometimes can be also used for teenagers. The group shares ideas and stories on a topic such as the funeral. A large piece of paper is then placed on the floor. It is large enough for each member of the bereavement group to have enough space to draw or paint the "weather." In this case the "weather" is the way they felt on the day of the funeral or on the first day back to school after the loss of a loved one. The "weather" they draw can be a way to bring their inner emotions to the forefront. This approach allows the participants to use a technique other than oral discussion, which may be uncomfortable for many. It allows a free expression of feelings in an artistic way. It is also helpful because it is a shared task. Many people who have a death in the family feel isolated in their grief. Just being together with members of a bereavement group helps them feel that they are not alone.

The Story

A story is chosen with a common theme that the participants in the bereavement group can relate to. They might also watch a videotape on a subject of common interest. After the story has been read, or the videotape has been shown, the participants in the group are given an opportunity to discuss what they felt during the course of the narrative. They may also talk about the feelings expressed by the protagonist as well as their own feelings. This method provides an opportunity for individuals in the bereavement group to talk about their own circumstances. The main objective of this technique is to have the individuals understand that others can feel the same way as they do, and that the feelings they have are not irrational. It is also helpful to allow participants to identify with the main character on an emotional level without taking the risk of identifying their own feelings in front of a group.

The Mandala or Colored Wheel

A piece of paper with a circle on it is placed in front of each person in the bereavement group. Everyone is given magic markers, colored pencils, or pastels. Everyone is asked to make a list of the emotions they are feeling. They are then asked to color code each emotion. Sad could be blue; guilt could be green; anger could be red; joy could be yellow; and so on. The teenagers are then told to color a portion of the circle with the emotion that they are feeling. This technique gives the participants an opportunity to get in touch visually with how they are feeling. If they see a circle with one half colored red and one tenth colored yellow, they can see for themselves that they are feeling a great deal of anger and little joy. They can keep this wheel and look back at it in, say, six months time to see if there are any changes in the way they feel. They can make a new wheel every so often to test for changes in their feelings. The wheel also allows another person, such as a counselor, to see the teen's feelings as well. It visually identifies where the teenager is at the moment. Does the color red always predominate, or does the teen change to another color?

More Helpful Ideas

There are many books available that will give bereaved survivors ideas on how to help themselves manage their grieving process. Here are some other useful tips and ideas.

⮒ Visualize feeling healthy and hold this vision in
your mind. Remember a time and place when you
felt happy and see that picture in your head. When
you are feeling sad and lonely, go to that memory
and relax.

⮒ Practice mental focusing. Try to keep your mind
free of thoughts and images. One way to practice
this is to stare at a candle. Keep staring at it until
you are free of thought. You can also do this by
humming a note like *om* and concentrating on the
sound. Your mind eventually relaxes.

⮒ Turn your attention to your breathing. When you
have feelings of anxiety and relaxation is neces-
sary, deep breathing is helpful.

1. Feel your breath go in and come out. Get in touch with
your breathing cycle.
2. Draw your breath in with a deep inhalation. Feel the
breath right down to your toes.
3. Hold your breath for a short duration of time.
4. Exhale forcefully.
5. Continue this exercise until you can almost see your
breath traveling the distance of your body.
6. Your breathing should be slow and you should practice
this during a quiet moment with your eyes closed.

↝ Music has a calming effect, depending on what songs you play. Find a number of songs that make you feel good about yourself. Play them when you need an uplift. Music may also be a way to connect with the deceased. Maybe your loved one had a favorite recording artist or piece of music or song. Playing it may help to keep the memory of your loved one alive.

↝ Surround yourself with nurturing people and friends. Avoid too much stress and conflict at this time. You want to have your life made easier, not more difficult or stressful. This may not be the time to overindulge yourself with committees or new projects. This may be the time to lay low until you feel in control enough to take on new projects.

↝ Join a group, such as a bereavement group, to share ideas. If you are unable to do so, join a group that you feel comfortable with, one that won't have too many expectations of you as you are emotionally healing. A bereavement group offers a time to connect with others who are feeling as you do. These groups are usually organized and run by counselors who have been trained in this area of expertise. Most teenagers like this kind of group process because it helps them to feel less alone. If there is no bereavement group in your area, joining a group of people who do charity work may serve the same purpose.

↝ Volunteer your time to help others. It may be helpful to work with children who need your guidance. You can learn from them and they in turn can learn from you. Working with the elderly can also be helpful. They have experienced loss and pain in their lives. Many are willing to share their stories and are willing to hear yours.

↝ Meditation, yoga, and other relaxation techniques will help to lessen your anxiety. It is also important to understand that the emotions you are feeling are normal and do not have to be masked all the time. Focusing yourself through meditation works when you are feeling great anxiety and you are having difficulty managing.

↝ Walk or run it out. Exercise and sports can be healthy both mentally and physically. Exercise has a way of unfocusing your mind for the moment. It is another way to help yourself heal. Some teenagers are not motivated to go back to their school teams because they feel saddened and don't feel that they can do their team justice. This may be true, but getting back to your sport may help in the grieving process. It can be a momentary escape and a release from the tension you have been experiencing.

↝ Take care of yourself. Eat, rest, and try to heal both your mind and body. Don't abuse yourself. Take care of yourself inwardly and outwardly. Looking and feeling good about yourself sometimes helps the inner you. Drinking alcohol and taking drugs are not the answer for inner peace. They may create their own inner hell. Before going to bed, avoid drinking caffeinated drinks such as coffee, tea, and soda. The deep breathing exercises could be helpful before you go to bed.

⇨ Make yourself laugh. Humor is also a way to help in the grieving process. Watching funny shows, videos, and reading humorous stories or the comics allows you to laugh again. Although some people feel guilty for laughing, it is very helpful for you to start feeling good about yourself again.

⇨ Talk about it. This is the time to talk to friends and help them to help you. If this is difficult, try a therapist, school counselor, family member, or member of the clergy. There are KIDS HELP phone lines that you can try. The people monitoring the calls can be supportive and direct you to further help.

⇨ Write your feelings down. Use a journal or diary to help you record your thoughts and emotions. Reflect on what you have written on a regular basis.

⇨ Keep a dream journal. Write down your dreams and nightmares. See if the messages your unconscious mind is sending you can be helpful in your day-to-day life.

⇨ Talk into a tape recorder. If writing is not your thing, just keeping a diary of your feelings by talking into a tape recorder can be beneficial.

⇨ Make a video. Sometimes just using the video camera to catch memories and putting these remembrances together can be helpful. Creating a narrative can also be therapeutic.

⇨ To further remember, write about incidents, the way the person looked, how his or her voice sounded, and so on. One fear that teenagers have is that they will forget the loved one.

↪ Take advantage of on-line bereavement groups. Exploring the Internet can also be helpful when you connect with others who have also just recently had a death in the family. It should be emphasized here that it is very important that you do not share personal information, such as your full name, address, school, and so on, so that you protect your identity. The on-line group should be a legitimate one, so it would be advisable to get help from a mental health agency in your area in choosing one. Sometimes just being able to talk to someone, without that person knowing everything about you, allows you to be less reserved.

↪ Visit a place that you find relaxing, comforting, and peaceful. This is your own special place. It could be a park, a church, a synagogue, a gallery, or a pond. It is a place where you can feel good about yourself.

↪ It is time to rebuild your relationships with your family. Try to spend some quality time with your family. You don't have to focus on the death of your loved one. Try focusing on the new dynamics. Playing a card game, doing a family puzzle, making a garden together, picking berries, or playing baseball outside are all activities that can allow new relationships to develop.

↝ Spend time alone. This may be the time to read books, work on your hobby, explore the Internet, or watch a video. It is fine to be on your own, but don't isolate yourself completely.

↝ Remember that it is all right to have feelings of sadness. These may come in waves. A thought, a symbol, or a smell may bring the memory of your loved one back to you. It is OK to feel sad.

↝ It is also time to look into the future. Try not to dwell in the past. Plan a day ahead, a week ahead, a month ahead, and then longer.

↝ Make a chart of your feelings. Look back from time to time and see how you are doing.

Emotions	Yes/No	Comments
Sad	____	
Angry	____	
Joy	____	
Guilty	____	
Depressed	____	
Fear	____	
Confused	____	
Sick	____	
Shocked	____	
Happiness	____	

Commemorate a shared loss. This can be done as part of a small group or as a school project. An activity can be planned to commemorate the death of a teacher or student. Others in the community can participate in the activity or the presentation. This gives further support to students who are grieving. You can plant a memory garden or a tree, make a quilt, paint a mural, or compose a song or a poem.

Step by Step

When teaching about the grieving process, the following stepladder can be used as a step-by-step approach to accepting loss and discovering the potential for growth from that loss. It is a diagram of the grieving process that starts with your own pain and takes you to the point where you are strong enough to help others.

The Steps to Recovery

#5 Recognizing the potential for growth from loss
#4 Helping ourselves, helping others through grief
#3 Seeing death as a special kind of loss
#2 Understanding grief as a natural response to loss
#1 Recognizing loss and seeing it as part of the life cycle

Each part of the ladder can be helpful for the bereavement counselor in assisting the survivor to recognize the different significant stages of loss. A counselor can help you identify where you are on the ladder and how you will move to the fifth rung. The following checklist, outlined by Dr. Alan Wolfelt in his book *Helping Children Cope with Grief,* can be helpful.

↝ Be a good observer. Respond to the teenager by maintaining eye contact and explore questions rather than give quick answers.

↝ Respond in an empathetic manner. Acknowledge and feel for what the teenager is going through or has gone through.

↝ Allow the teenager to express feelings and thoughts. Let the teenager communicate his or her depth of understanding rather than attempt to diagnose what the teenager is thinking and feeling.

↝ Respond in language that the teenager can understand. Use simple and direct language.

↝ Respond to the impact of events rather than to the events themselves. The teen's perceptions of reality are more important than reality itself.

↝ Respond in a voice, tone, and intensity that match the expression of the teenager.

↝ Recognize and respond to cues. Check the accuracy of what the teenager is reporting to you.

↝ Observe nonverbal behavior.

↝ Express feelings that are natural to the situation.

↝ Answer the teenager's questions.

↝ Be patient and available.

↝ Provide reassurance through action as well as words.

➥ Learn to feel at ease during silence. The teenager needs to talk at his or her own pace.

➥ Maintain a dialogue with the teenager about death as the opportunity arises. Do not wait for the teenager to tell all.

➥ Create a healthy relationship.

Select and adjust your procedures according to the individual teenager. No one fit is a perfect fit for all. Each person is an individual.

Violence in the Schools

The newspapers have been reporting more and more incidents of violence in North American schools. Television has been projecting the images of students during and after violent attacks from their peer groups. Teenagers are witnessing violence and some are the victims of violence. When students from around the world watch the kind of tragic events that occurred in such places as Littleton, Colorado, they have strong emotional reactions. They wonder whether shootings will occur in their town or school. They may identify with the victims and their families or even with the aggressors. They may also feel shock, anger, and sadness. When the world becomes an instant witness to violent attacks, teenagers desperately need to talk about their feelings. After a traumatic event has occurred in the school system, tragic-event counseling teams are usually called in to assist the survivors. The tragic-event team is a multidisciplinary group specially trained to deal with crises of this nature.

Teenagers who have either witnessed violence firsthand or who have been victims themselves or are associated in some way with tragic events need to tell their stories. They want to make sense of what has happened and why it has happened. They need the opportunity to talk about the violence and about what they have witnessed, and they need to feel safe again. Teenagers do not generally dwell on their own deaths. When a tragic event occurs, teens are suddenly faced with the realization of their own immortality. This one major event throws them into utter confusion. They require coping strategies to assist them on the road to recovery.

The crises teenagers experience may cause them to look at life differently. They don't take things for granted anymore. At the graduation ceremony in Littleton, Colorado, the speeches focused on appreciating the value of life. The attitudes of the students had changed, and the tragedy had led some to an increased maturity.

> *In my experience coping with this event thus far, I have reflected upon my own way of life and decided a few changes are necessary. I, as a rule, am tense and forget to enjoy simple pleasures because I am so busy. I also tend to stress out and get upset over relatively minute details. Lauren Townsend, my friend who died in the library at C.H.S., was a very studious and hardworking girl, yet she also found time to fit in pleasure, without stressing herself too much. I hope to learn from her example, knowing all too well how quickly life can escape us.* —Pam Glazner, student at Columbine High School, Littleton, Colorado (quoted in the *New York Times*, May 23, 1999)

In a traumatic situation, teenagers will go through stages of grieving somewhat similar to those we have already described. The first stage is the shock or frozen fright stage. It takes a few moments for the reality of an event like a shooting to sink in. "This couldn't be happening here. I can't believe it." Teenagers may blame themselves for not reacting sooner to the situation. After the event they may experience feelings of guilt. "If I had reacted sooner, I could have saved someone." During this stage the physical reactions of teens are usually heightened. The heart will beat at a faster pace, breathing will become shallow and rapid, and there may be a heightened sensory awareness of sights, sounds, and smells. This sensory stimulation may deeply impact the brain. Sensory stimuli, such as a certain smell, can remind the teen of the event even years later.

At the moment of the tragedy, the teenager may be in a dreamlike state. The emotions are deadened, and this provides a protective cushion around the individual until he or she is ready to absorb the truth. It is hard for the teenager to believe that these events are happening at this point in time.

Teenagers will react differently in a time of extreme crisis. Sometimes the body just reacts without one's control. A person can urinate, defecate, or vomit. Afterward the person may feel embarrassed by these intense reactions. It is important to understand that these reactions are normal. Young people going to war for the first time may feel so scared that they wet themselves. A person going through a traumatic event may feel confused, frustrated, angered, outraged, or terrified. After the event, still in a state of shock, the teenager may be so wired that he or she may not be able to rest or sleep. After a period of time, the teenager's body surrenders to fatigue and eventually he or she sleeps. When the teenager awakens, the events are part of history. Sometimes teens feel guilty. "How could I sleep when this just occurred?" Counselors must stress that both this excitement and subsequent fatigue are normal at this point.

It is important that the counselor not say "You have to get on with your life." The teen is not ready to hear or absorb this. On the other hand, members of the community feel the need to get on with their lives. They want to feel safe once again. They may hold a memorial service very soon after the tragedy. Many people are not yet ready for the memorial service. They have not yet emotionally recognized that the person has died. The memorial service does allow people to come together and grieve together. It is a time where teens can hold each other and let their tears flow.

Teenagers may not want to talk with an adult after a tragic event. There is a strong need for privacy at this age. Crisis prevention teams recognize this and try to use techniques that allow teenagers to talk while respecting their rights. It is important for people to understand that traumatic events such as the Littleton, Colorado, shootings may be just a news piece for the rest of the world, but these teenagers and their families have a long and difficult grieving process ahead of them and may need some help along the way.

Closing Thoughts

Death has many lessons to teach us. The teenagers we interviewed were all at different stages in the grieving process. Some had less than a year to reflect on their feelings, and others had the distance of a number of years. Each handled their grieving differently. Each had unique feelings about the maturity the experience had brought them. They each had their own special words of wisdom to share with their peer group. Some were fatalistic. What had happened, happened. They did not feel in control.

You are born, you do something, you die. In between you may have fun. Nothing ever stays. It sucks. What's the sense? — Krystal

Other teenagers felt the need to appreciate every moment of life. They understood that at any moment their lives could be interrupted and altered by a tragic event like a death of a loved one. They wanted to advise others to be mindful of one's words and actions.

I see how friends treat brothers and sisters. I want them to stop being so mean. What would happen if something happened the next day? Everyone has to find their own way of coping. They must find their own way. — Kelvin

Tell everyone who you love that you love them because you might not be able to tell them again. Don't have regrets about what you did or didn't do. — Karla

Everyone reacts differently. Watch what you say to everyone. This may be the last time you talk to them. — Sarah

Let people close to you know that you love them. When they are gone, it is too late. — Tasha

Throughout the grieving process, teenagers may experience emotions they have never had to deal with before. It is difficult for them to deal with their own pain, anger, and fear. It is important for teens to get in touch with their feelings and not attempt to hide them when a tragedy occurs.

A lot of guys hold back their tears. It's better and easier to let it all out. Try to remember as much as you can. The more memories, the easier it is to get through it. Talk to your family to keep the memories. Talk to other family members, such as aunts and uncles, about your loved one's childhood. It helped me get closer to mom. I was happy that I knew something more about her life before the short time I knew her. — Matthew

State your feelings. Don't commit suicide yourself. I have a fear of death. I don't want family or friends

to die. I would not be able to take it. The more death, the worse you feel. — Alex

Don't hide your feelings. Let people help you. Don't be afraid to move on. Go out and set goals for yourself. Get on with your life. Mom would have wanted me to succeed and be happy. I will be successful for mom and for me. Don't give up on yourself. Believe in yourself, be positive, although this may be hard. Get involved. Help others. Be positive. I buy carnations every year in honor of my mom and to help support the American Cancer Society. High school and college were very difficult for me, and my graduation ceremonies were very special events in my life. I prayed that she was looking down at me and was there. I wanted her to see me at my prom and getting accepted to university. I wanted her to be here for all the stages of my life. — Tasha

Some teenagers, based on their personal experiences, highly recommended counseling, whether it is on an individual basis or in a bereavement group. Each person who received some bereavement counseling felt differently about it, but most felt better.

I recommend counseling when needed. I went to a bereavement group. For some people it works. Talking about it helps, especially with a friend. I have dealt with it. I have dealt with my emotions in a positive manner. You need to let it out or it will get to you. — Kelvin

If you can't handle it, it's good to see a therapist.
— Matthew

See a doctor. Go to a bereavement group. Talk to someone, a friend, a parent, a relative, a vice-principal, whenever you are feeling sad. — Alex

Don't let people tell you how you feel. If you want counseling, get it, but I don't want it. Maybe you don't want someone to know how you feel. — Sarah

The bereavement group is helpful because you know you are not the only one. — Nina

Some teenagers tried to understand the reason behind the death. Could there possibly be some meaning, some reason for the death to have occurred? Should they be learning something from the grieving experience? Most teenagers felt that their lives had changed remarkably after going through the experience of having someone so close to them die.

I went to church a couple of years ago. Church is comforting. I talked to God. I accept that things happen and rely on God to take care of her. Friends and family are my main comforts. You don't know how you will feel until it happens to you. You cannot imagine. Be thankful for what you have. Move on with your life. — Meghan

Everything happens for a reason. God chooses strong people. Hindus believe in souls. If I do bad on

tests, it means I have to work a little harder. Everything now happens for a reason. I am more positive. I am a stronger person. So much has come out of me that would not have happened. People look up to me, take my advice, because of what I have been through. I have gained so much. Stand up with a smile on your face. — Nina

The teenagers we interviewed shared their stories in order to help other teens going through their own grieving process. Never once did they say that they went through the process easily. It was a long, hard struggle. For some it still remains a struggle. The therapists and religious leaders we interviewed felt that teenagers required time and support to work through their grief. Teens need to understand the emotions they are experiencing. It is recommended that teenagers talk to someone—a friend, a therapist, a member of the clergy, a family member, or a counselor from school. Remember, you are not alone in your feelings.

The woman who looked around her village and tried to find a family not touched by death could not find one. Death is part of living. Grieving is important as a special reminder of how unique your loved one was to you.

Glossary

AIDS Acquired immunodeficiency syndrome, a disease in which one's immune system is unable to fight off infections.

amphetamines Central nervous system stimulants.

bereavement The state of being lonely and sad because someone has died.

cocaine A drug that if taken internally or sniffed acts as a stimulant. It can cause addiction.

coroner A public officer whose most usual task is to hold inquiries into the causes of accidental or suspicious deaths.

CPR Cardiopulmonary resuscitation, an emergency method of clearing the breathing passage.

cremate To reduce to ashes by burning.

deceased A person who has died.

denial Refusal to admit that something is true or has really happened.

depression A period of despair or sadness, sometimes marked by lack of activity.

empathetic Having the ability to enter into the feelings or spirit of others.

fatalistic Accepting one's fate with stoicism. A disposition to accept every event or condition as inevitable.

funeral The burial, cremation, or final disposal of the body of a dead person, together with accompanying services.

Ganesh Ganesh in the Hindu religion represents that aspect of the Supreme Lord who ensures righteousness, removes hurdles, and ensures success in human endeavors. Ganesh is symbolized by a human form with an elephant head.

grief The many feelings you experience when you lose something or someone very important to you. Deep and painful sorrow.

hypocrisy Insincerity.

immortality Living forever, never dying.

irrational Unreasonable.

MADD Mothers Against Drunk Driving.

mortality The condition of being mortal or subject to death.

mourning The act of showing sadness or sorrow over someone's death.

naivete Simplicity, lacking worldly experience.

profound Requiring deep thought.

psychologist A specialist in the scientific study of human behavior.

reincarnation The belief that after physical death the soul lives a new life in a different body.

ritual A prescribed form or method for the performance of a religious or solemn ceremony.

Sabbath The seventh day of the week, or from Friday to Saturday evening, as a day of rest and worship observed by Jewish and Christian peoples.

shiva In Judaism, a seven-day period of mourning.

shock A sudden or severe agitation of the mind or emotions.

shrine A tomb, chapel, or other place held sacred because of the presence of religious relics.

suicide When someone ends his or her own life.

vulnerable Capable of being hurt or damaged.

wake A time for people to see a dead person before he or she is buried.

Where to Go for Help

In the United States

Center for Substance Abuse Treatment
800-662-HELP

Gang Hotline
800-900-GANG

Gay and Lesbian Youth Line
800-347-TEEN

National AIDS Hotline
800-342-2437

National Runaway Switchboard
800-621-4000

Nine Lines (teens in crisis with family or in school)
800-999-9999

In the United States and Canada

Al-Anon/Al-A-Teen
800-344-2666

Children of the Night Hotline
800-551-2666

Mothers Against Drunk Driving (MADD)
800-438-MADD

National Child Abuse Hotline
800-422-4453

National Organization for Victim Assistance (NOVA)
800-879-6682

Nationwide Hospice Organization
800-658-8898

Youth Crisis Hotline
800-448-4463

In Canada

Kids Help Phone Line
800-668-6868

Web Sites

The Child's Loss
http://gladstone.uoregon.edu/~dvb/perrylos.htm

GriefNet
http://www.griefnet.demon.co.uk

Kids Help Phone Line
http:kidshelp.sympatico.ca

WEBster: Death, Dying, and Grief Resources
http://www.katsden.com/death/index.htm/

For Further Reading

DiGiulio, Robert and Rachel Kranz. *Straight Talk About Death and Dying.* New York: Facts on File, Inc., 1995.

Eaton Heegaard, Marge. *Coping with Death and Grief.* Minneapolis: Lerner Publishing Co., 1990.

Fitzgerald, Helen. *The Mourning Handbook.* New York: A Fireside Book, 1994.

Frigo, V.D. Fisher, and M. Cook. *You Can Help Someone Who's Grieving.* New York: Penguin, 1996.

Grollman, Earl. *Bereaved Children and Teens.* Boston: Beacon Press, 1995.

Harris, Maxine. *The Loss That Is Forever: The Lifelong Impact of the Early Death of a Mother or Father.* New York: Plume, 1995.

Kübler-Ross, Elisabeth, and Mal Warshaw. *To Live Until We Say Goodbye.* Englewood Cliffs, NJ: Prentice–Hall, 1978.

McIlwraith, Hamish. *Coping with Bereavement.* England: Oneworld, 1998.

O'Toole, Donna. *Growing Through Grief.* Burnsville, NC: Mountain Rainbow Publications, 1989.

Richter, Elizabeth. *Losing Someone You Love: When a Brother or Sister Dies.* New York: G. P. Putnam and Sons, 1986.

Saynor, John Kennedy. *Goodbye Buddy.* Toronto: Turner & Porter Funeral Directors Ltd., 1990.

White, James R. Grieving: *Our Path Back to Peace.* Minneapolis: Bethany House Publishers, 1997.

Wolfelt, Alan. *Helping Children Cope with Grief.* Muncie, IN: Accelerated Development Inc., 1983.

Wolfelt, Alan. *Sarah's Journey.* Fort Collins: Center for Loss and Life Transition, 1992.

Wolfelt, Alan. *Understanding Grief: Helping Yourself Heal.* Muncie, IN: Accelerated Development Inc., 1992.

Index